# PRIDE

## the Greatest Sin?

# PRIDE

## the Greatest Sin?

Snehprabha Kanagaraj

TATE PUBLISHING
AND ENTERPRISES, LLC

# Synopsis: Pride— the Greatest Sin?

Is there anyone on this earth who can say, "I am not proud"? Everyone is proud of something or the other but very few people experience destruction caused by pride which they can actually acknowledge. The reason is because pride can invade us with or without our consent or knowledge. Again this is a story of my life showing how pride can take away all the blessings of our lives without our knowledge; and if we do not acknowledge it soon enough, how our lives can become miserable. Usually when we do something wrong, there is someone who can make us realize or feel that eventually we are wrong. But harboring pride that causes destruction leading to all other sins is one thing that only God can make us realize; as such I feel pride can be considered as the greatest sin, even though there is no small or great sin, however we argue, because no matter what, sin is a sin. Would you agree?

# Vision for This Book

My vision for this book is to try to help people to self-diagnose to see if the so-called pride is invading, or has invaded, or will invade their lives without their consent or knowledge and to stop themselves from falling victim to this great root of sin, which could destroy lives and keep them away from the blessings God has kept for them. It can be stopped at any stage by only one way, and that is by turning to our living God—Jesus—who is the perfect example of humbleness. Once we surrender ourselves to him, his word will come true in our lives which says—*By humility and the fear of Lord are riches and honor and life.* (Proverbs 22:4).

# Acknowledgments and Preface

"With God I am hero, without God I am zero," is one of my favorite quotations ever since I experienced God in my life. Thanks to him who has given me thoughts to share; without his help I couldn't have written even a single sentence.

I thank him for my life's experiences even though they seemed painful at the time, but they have taught me great lessons. Thank God for everyone who has come across my life, even the ones whom I hated at that time. It seemed so unfair as many times I was wrongly accused by others even though I did not do anything wrong. Little did I know at that time that we need a pharaoh to reach the promised land. I am thankful for such people through whom I have learned some valuable lessons in some way or the other. I thank him for my children without whom I could not have learned anything. I want to thank God for my husband who always supports me in everything I do.

I want to thank Sister Manisha Patidar for her contribution of thoughts which always seem to agree with my own thoughts. I thank Mr. Sanjay Franklin for his willingness to help me whenever I needed his help especially with the computer. I am thankful to God for Mr. Vijay Kumar for his input, his ideas and having shared his thoughts throughout the book. I am very grateful to Reverend John Pappachan and Reverend Rajan George and some other preachers whose messages have always confirmed my thoughts which I had written way before they spoke. It always seemed like what I had written is my experience based on their thoughts—often I wondered, "Is that the work of the Holy Spirit?" I never talk or tell them what I write yet they seem to talk on those topics, giving me the confirmation that I need. I wonder how different people, without discussing with each other, have pretty much the same thoughts, same outlook, same understanding. One such topic was *pride*.

Everybody can have pride but this book tells about the pride in my life, its consequences, how it led to destroy my life's blessings, and how difficult and long it took for me to realize what I had lost, and then how God had restored much more than what I had lost once I realized and humbled myself before him. Now it makes me feel to understand little bit as to how sixty-six books of the Bible must have been written by different people with different backgrounds over different time frames yet contains the same message of salvation throughout. It is still a mystery to me but then again anything that has something to do with God is always a mystery.

As it says in Ecclesiastes 3:11, "also he hath set the world in their heart, so that no man can find out the work that God maketh from the beginning to the end." Is there anyone on earth who can say, "Yes, I understand God"? Many times he reveals things and gives us the guidance to walk in his ways, but to understand God it is just impossible for mortals. So let us try not to do what we can never do but instead just submit ourselves in his hands and believe that he will lead us in the perfect direction to our perfect destination in life. Just relax and enjoy the free ride filled with heaven's choicest blessings that he is willing to give and gives to everyone who is humble enough to believe and obey *him*.

"As long as you are proud you cannot know God. A proud man is always looking down on thing and people: and, of course, as long as you are looking down you cannot see something that is above you."

—C. S. Lewis, *Mere Christianity*

"God allows us to experience the low points of life in order to teach us lessons that we could learn in no other way."

—C. S. Lewis

"For pride is spiritual cancer: it eats up the very possibility of love, or contentment, or even common sense."

—C. S. Lewis, *Mere Christianity*

# Contents

Introduction ................................................................... 19

Everything Is Vanity! ..................................................... 27
Salvation Is Free but the Rest Needs to Be Paid ...... 55
Knowing His Will Calls for Accountability ............. 67
What Is So Special in the Name of Jesus? ............... 83
Pride Can Invade with or without Our Consent ..... 91
What Do We Need in the End? ............................. 103
Choosing to Surrender to the Wrong Master! ....... 115
Does God Talk Only If We Speak in Tongues? ..... 125
Godly Love versus Worldly Love .......................... 135
Judging Others Can Give Good Results Too ......... 141
Blessings and Sufferings Accompany
     God's Love ...................................................... 147
Accepting and Doing God's Will .......................... 155
Faith That My Son Taught Me ............................. 161
God Loves Humility ............................................ 171

Index ................................................................... 187
About the Author ................................................ 195

# Introduction

"Pride goeth before destruction" (Proverbs 16:18), one of the wise sayings from the wisest person on this earth like whom was never before and never will be as what God had said—Yes, I am talking about King Solomon, the one whom God glorified like no other, to whom he had promised that he will never ever again give that much wisdom to any other human being on this earth. Can you imagine that? The creator of this universe is promising to a mere human being that there will never ever be a person again after him who will be much wiser than him in the generations before and in the generations after (1 Kings 3:12). If I had received a promise like that then I cannot even imagine how it might have made me feel at that time; probably it would have made me feel very proud of myself. Even just the fact that the creator of this universe had spoken to me would have made me so proud. Wish I was there to ask King Solomon what and how he had felt at that time, that moment? Was he happy, stunned, amazed, surprised, excited—did he even have a word to describe what he had felt? Did it invite *pride in his heart*, which is considered *sin*? (Proverbs 21:4)

What is pride anyway? Most of us know the dictionary meaning of this word—it is nothing but a feeling of elation to think highly of self. Actually it is very difficult to define *pride* in words, it is something that we can point out very easily in other people. Pride is the beginning of sin which if we fail to acknowledge can lead to all sins—including the sin of unbelief. Pride is a rebellion against God because it makes us to glorify ourselves instead of glorifying him. The Bible talks more about the consequences of harboring pride than emphasizing on defining the word. Pride is an attitude that stops us from doing what we would otherwise do. It separates us from God and it is something only he can convict us about. Sister Manisha, our church member, words *pride* as a highway to hell, which is amusing yet fatally true; in fact I almost considered that for the title of this book during our discussion on pride.

When people invent or come up with something new—something extraordinary—they get so excited, happy, and tend to become proud. They think highly of themselves thinking that they did something that nobody else even thought of doing, thus dream of becoming a millionaire or billionaire. Me too, as many of us would probably be; many times feel that way. One of my hobbies is painting—I love painting. Though I have not painted many paintings, whenever I did paint something, especially landscapes, which is my passion, if those turn out to be beautiful to look at and when people say those are beautiful paintings, even though I know myself how many mistakes and flaws that can be found in those paintings, still it makes me feel so happy and proud of myself. I was thinking how King Solomon must have felt when God gave him that promise of wisdom. And then not only that, he also gave him the riches and wealth beyond his expectation. 1 Kings 3:12–13 says, "I have given thee a wise and an understanding heart; so that there was none like thee before thee, neither after thee shall any arise like unto thee. And I have also given thee which thou hast not asked, both riches and honor:"

Wow! What a promise! Often I wonder how King Solomon could not feel proud of himself. Even though it says that his heart had turned away from God when he got old and that he did not keep God's commandments, still I give him a lot of credit for having that self-control for so many years in spite of what he had and what he was blessed by God. But as I read his books, especially the book of

Ecclesiastes in the Bible, it seems like there came a point in his life when he felt that everything in this world—all the wisdom, wealth, health—was vanity. The only lasting thing was the fear of God, and he seemed to understand the fact that the need to obey him is the only thing in life that would bring satisfaction in anybody's life.

The wisest person on earth did the dumbest things in life. Maybe it was his inquisitiveness that made him experience everything in his life, good or bad; maybe he knew the outcome of his actions before he even did them, or maybe it was his pride that might have stepped in his life before he could realize. Or maybe it was his pride that led him to destruction and lose his blessings, as even though the Bible talks about him realizing his mistakes, yet it does not talk about him being humble enough to ask forgiveness from God. Perhaps that is the reason he wrote so much about pride in his books. Even though in the last chapter of Ecclesiastes and in conclusion he says that the only thing that matters is the fear of God and advises people to obey him, but the question I ask myself is: Did he do that, and if he did, why was it not mentioned? What was he thinking? Did he think it is too late to repent or ask for forgiveness? Or did he still have pride which made him not to humble himself before God? Or did he just assume that God will not forgive him? Wish I had the chance to talk to the wisest, most glorious person who existed on earth. I just want to know for myself how I might have felt to encounter him to ask him some simple questions like: How could he disobey someone who had given him everything, with whom he had personal encounter, whom he knew was God himself? How could he not have his fear? What was he thinking? Did he have pride in his heart, which made him lose all the blessings? It is difficult for me to comprehend, but again when I think what pride can do then I have to believe anything can happen to anybody, even to the wisest, most disciplined person on earth.

Maybe that is why the Bible says the wisest people on earth are actually the ones who keep seeking God; in other words, to be foolish in earthly terms is far better than being wise. It says in Proverbs 26:12, "Do you see persons wise in their own eyes? There is more hope for fools than for them." And 1 Corinthians 3:18–19 says, "If you think that you are wise in this age, you should become fools so that you may become wise. For the wisdom of this world is foolishness with God." Before you read any further, think of becoming wise in the eyes of God. If you do then maybe you need not read any further, just pick up the Bible and start reading. It will teach you a lot of things that I have learned the hard way in my life. Or else you can read the journey of my life and enjoy the roller-coaster ride that pride took me, teaching me the lessons that I have learned, which, by the way, I am sure I will never forget the rest of my life.

I earnestly pray that people will not fall victim to this great sin, which can surely destroy anybody's life and steal God's choicest blessings. Of course there is no small or great sin, for sin is a sin. But why I personally call this as a great sin is because I feel it not only leads us to commit all other sins but it also stops us from listening or seeing. If you have pride, you don't need anything else to be away from God. The worst part is that it makes us feel as if nothing is wrong committing this sin; but the moment we come to our senses and we realize that we have committed this sin, then we understand that everything is wrong. Then we won't believe that we actually committed this sin without knowing and facing the consequences that we would have avoided otherwise had we known.

The Scriptures does not word *pride* as sin literally, but it leads us to imply that it is a sin—rather the root cause of all sins leading to destruction, which no doubt God hates. But again the Scriptures are written and rewritten and translated from different languages many times, so it is difficult to say whether or not pride was ever considered as sin—

or greatest sin—until the Holy Spirit reveals that to you. As such, I will leave up to you all if you would consider this as the greatest sin.

May God open your eyes as you read through this book so that pride will not destroy your lives. It is very easy and simple to stay away from this great sin just by inviting Jesus to live in you, who is the perfect example of humbleness. If you don't agree with me then just try, see for yourselves, experience the transformation that will take place in you by having Jesus in your lives, the blessings that you will receive which you will be longing to share thereafter with everyone you meet. You will then see his promise coming true in your lives according to his word—By humility and fear of the Lord are riches, honor and life. (Proverbs 22:4).

The things we consider that are bad for us, we may not actually perceive that maybe those were in fact good for us, as we only see the good and bad aspects of those things in that moment, not in the long run. But God sees way ahead of us.

# Everything Is Vanity!

I had lived a worldly life for forty-plus years before it dawned on me that nothing in this world really mattered—only after which I could understand what King Solomon had meant when he made one statement, "Everything is vanity." I had enjoyed a lot in life in worldly terms. My understanding was that God is the one who gave us life to enjoy, so enjoy it. It never occurred to me to think why he had made both good and bad things, why he created both beautiful and ugly things, why he gave human beings brain to think and choice to choose. It would have been a lot easier for God to create everything right and then make us do what he wanted us to do. But he did not do it that way because God wanted his creation to come to him on their own free will, to appreciate his goodness thus love him.

Someone has written a book titled *Why Bad Things Happen to Good People*. It seems to be an interesting book, which, by the way, I did not yet get a chance to read. Even then I can say very confidently by my own experience that bad things do not happen to good people. Again, what do we mean by "good people"? Are these people the ones who always do good to others? Do not steal? Do not lie? Do not commit murder, etc.? If that is the definition then I am afraid I do not agree. Scripture says in Proverbs 21:2–4, *"All deeds are right in the sight of the doer but the Lord weighs the heart. To do righteousness and justice is more acceptable to the Lord than sacrifice. Haughty eyes and a proud heart—the lamp of the wicked—are sin"*. So doing good works or sacrificing ourselves is not enough especially when we harbor pride in our hearts. For me "good people" means "right people," and right people can only be right when they obtain the righteousness of God, which can only come through not by our works but by God's grace, as it says in Ephesians 2:8–9, "For by grace are ye saved through faith; and that not of yourselves: it is the gift of God: Not of works, lest any man should boast."

People who are right with God also can face bad things in their lives, maybe more bad things than others. They might even be tempted to say, "Why are bad things happening to us? Why us?"

We then just have to trust in God more even though it may not seem fair or right at that time. The things we consider that are bad for us, we may not actually perceive that maybe those were in fact good for us as we only see the good and bad aspect of those things in that moment, not in the long run. But God sees way ahead of us and then when we reach the time that he was looking way before, we finally acknowledge that whatever had happened at that time was indeed good for us. It is not easy to look where God is looking because we are born blind; or if we are not then we are near-sighted—we are not programmed to see the future. That does not mean we can never open our eyes—that's where God comes in. He can certainly reveal things and his plans for us for which we need to establish our relationship with him. We need to make sure he feels that we can be trusted and we have enough time to spend with him to know his secrets, or in other words talk to him frequently. It's the same with us—we don't just go and reveal our secrets to total strangers, right? We do that only after we build good relationships with people, spend time with them, and make sure they can be trusted to keep our secrets.

One day I was listening to Johnny Lever's testimony—one of the great comedian actors of Bollywood who had confessed that ever since he had a personal encounter with God, had accepted Jesus as his personal savior, his life has been transformed. Now he preaches and shares his testimony everywhere. In one of his sermons he had said, "We are born blind. We remain blind from birth till death until we choose to open our eyes to see the *light*—who is Jesus." In the New Testament in the Bible, John 8:12 says, "I am the light of the world: he that followeth me shall not walk in darkness, but shall have the light of life." So when we see that light, that is when our eyes are open, we then begin to actually live a life that is meaningful to us and others. We then get blessed and also become a source of blessing for people around us. Many people go to their graves blindfolded as they choose not to open their eyes to see the light, many times knowingly. Again what stops them from seeing is—pride.

It was very difficult for me to choose and trust in that light also especially when I felt bad things were happening to me. Felt it was not fair. I thought, *How could God let those things happen to me especially when he knows that I choose to believe in him, accept him as my God?* But my attitude changed when I started seeing things through his eyes. Everything happens for a reason. We may not have all the answers because our understanding has limitations. It is his promise. Romans 8:28 says, "And we know that all things work together for good to them that love God, to them who are the called according to his purpose." Those who believe in that promise see that happening in their lives. I have experienced that in my life, so now I can say with confidence that bad things will never happen to me again. We just have to believe that if we submit ourselves to God then those bad things will turn out to be good for us. Ever since Jesus has convinced me of his existence by doing what I had required of him, I have decided to be his follower, follow his teachings in the Bible not just by reading but also hearing from him directly as I read, more so now after experiencing him at personal level.

I had traveled a lot, seen beautiful places in India as well as in the US, enjoyed with people whom I really liked to be with; even after marriage there was not a dull moment in my life. People say marriage is the end of our life's journey, with which personally I disagree. Because it is only then we learn to live with others in a close relationship than any other relationship, so I feel our lives actually begin only after marriage. We learn to accept the weakness and strength of another human being if we don't give room for pride. There is so much excitement, adventures, love, sorrows, disappointments—we get to experience all the emotions that the creator has created for human beings to experience. I do have to say, though, marriage without God does not last too long. I am talking about true happiness in a marriage or, for that matter, in any relationship. We need God's love in us to overcome pride in order to remain in any relationship.

Anyway, like for many of us, for me also, marriage was a big adventure with a lot of roller-coaster rides. As the sayings go, "Life is too short," or "Time waits for no man," I did not want to waste any time in life. I was running—just running to catch something that was unknown to me. I wanted to take advantage of every moment, wanted to enjoy life without knowing what that word "enjoy" truly meant to me. Every day that I and my husband were off from work, we would plan to do something exciting. We used to drive a lot, since my husband loved to drive. As such there was not a single day when we were not out on the road seeing the most beautiful places in the United States.

I had to come to the United States after my marriage in India as my husband lives here. Even though I always used to say, "Be Indian, buy Indian," I somehow ended up marrying an American citizen but still who was from India. People say marriages are made in heaven, maybe ours was too, as we both come from two different places, two different backgrounds. How we met each other also seems like a very mysterious coincidence. I never thought or wanted to leave India but I ended up doing that. I am sure most of us might have heard that old saying, "Man proposes and God disposes." It does not matter how much we plan something; if it is not in God's agenda then it will never happen. Even though my heart is still very much Indian, I have learned to appreciate many things of Americans. I have come to accept the fact that there are good and bad things wherever people are involved—whether it is in America, India, or any other country. Now I do not regret coming to the United States because now I know it was God's plan for me. He wanted me to know his will and him at a personal level which I would never have done if I had stayed back in India.

It took twenty-plus years to see what God was trying to show me. I don't think anybody could have been more blind than me. I was too stubborn and was just refusing to see the promised land that God had in store for me because of the refusal to accept pride that was in me.

I had seen the most beautiful, breathtaking sceneries in the United States. I remember having seen those beautiful sceneries as postcards which we used to get as greeting cards for Christmas or as calendars when we were very young back home in India as my father used to have connections with foreigners because of his work. I never thought or even dreamed of seeing those sceneries in person. Now when I think about those sceneries, I recall one of my dad's remarks that he had made while traveling when he visited us the first time after our marriage in the US. He had said, "Everything is beautiful here but dead." It was amusing at that time but also true in a way because back home in India if we had any kind of greenery, mostly it would be something edible, something useful, not just beautiful to look at; maybe that is the reason my dad used the word "dead."

Anyway, the best of my most beautiful places was Niagara Falls, which still is today. Most people whom I know like to view the falls from the Canadian side—it is no doubt a beautiful view, I do agree, commonly known as "Horseshoe Falls," but personally I like to view the falls from the US side because from the US side we can not only view the falls but actually feel the falls as we are allowed to go almost to the top where the falls start. We can experience the majestic wonder of God's work firsthand. My husband and I often spent time there frequently. My husband does not really like to get wet yet he would do that for me. Even though I appreciate what he does, still sometimes it irritates me knowing that he is doing something he does not like to do. It actually shows the depth of his love for me—shows how far somebody can go to make someone else happy. I, on the other hand, didn't do any such thing in return, and to top it off I didn't feel anything wrong with that. Whatever I did I felt it was the right thing and I was quite proud of myself, which I was not willing to acknowledge.

People always treated me as very special for no particular reason, especially after I had believed in Christ and accepted him to be the living God whom I came to know personally as a teenager. I was so sure of God then that he would answer all my prayers, protect me from all the dangers, grant all my requests at all times. I was kind of an atheist before that as I was refusing to believe in God or any god. I never wanted to believe because I used to see and hear so many crimes happening in God's name or for religion's sake. But once I was convinced of his existence, I knew no one in the world could have succeeded in convincing me to believe otherwise. I had so much confidence and faith in God that he will take care of me no matter where I was or what I did. That overconfidence in myself brought in me the pride that I would not, could not, and did not acknowledge for a long time.

What I did not know at that time was that I was still serving two masters, as I never read scriptures then as I read now, except some of my favorite verses here and there. Still I was justifying myself that it was all right to do that, whereas in the Bible in the New Testament, Matthew 6:24 clearly says,

"No man can serve two masters." But then I always argued with everybody about everything, even with God, as at that time I was not having conversations as I have now, so it always happened that I ended up winning, thus justifying myself that what I was doing was indeed right. I would not listen to any-body anyway—so people usually never argued with me but instead just gave in and agreed with me rather than waste their time talking to convince me of something that they knew will not be able to convince me. I then, of course, took that in the wrong sense as to that I was right after all.

After I had got honor roll in my tenth grade, which was my requirement from God to believe in his existence, I had found myself changed dra-matically. I had believed that there is a real liv-ing God—Jesus—who will never leave me, who can perform miracles for me if I needed them, whom I can depend on for everything. Who was once known as a shy, quiet, innocent girl was not there anymore. I had become bold and beautiful, as one television show is named after. I was proud of myself—my looks, my talents, my achievements (even though they were not many)—just because of only one reason; that the creator of this universe had listened to me, had answered my prayer, and had shown himself to me. Just think about that. How and why wouldn't I take pride in that? I was not afraid of anything or anybody; I was willing to take any kind of risk in life. I had childlike faith then—so innocent, so real—nobody in the world could convince me to think that anything bad can happen to me because the God whom I had experienced, I knew is extraordinary; knew that he will take care of me no matter what, but what I did not know then was that God also expects something from us. He expects simple things from us like obedience, faithfulness, humbleness, forgiveness, etc. But the thing was that I was not aware of God's expectations from me at that time, that is why I think even though I did things that were not right in his sight, still he continued to bless me and protect me, which I took for granted as I found favor with everyone and everything.

I was a babe in Christ who did not know that I do have to grow up. God does not want us to be babies throughout our lives. He does not want us to drink milk for the rest of our lives but wants us to eat solid food. 1 Corinthians 3:2 said, " I have fed you with milk, and not with meat: for hitherto ye were not able to bear it." What God was trying to tell me then was that he was feeding me milk because I was then not ready for solid food; I did not understand at that time, but now I do understand. Again it is like parent-child relationship; we do not want our children to be children all their lives, we want them to grow right; and if they do not grow then we know it is not normal and we try to provide everything that will help them grow. Same thing with God—if he sees we are not growing according to his growth chart after becoming his children, then he will try to provide us with everything that will help us grow.

For me, I did not have anybody to give me the right direction especially since no one knew of the hunger that I had as I had not shared with anybody my experience, plus, as I had mentioned earlier, I would not have listened to anybody anyway. I was quite content with what I had experienced with the knowledge that I had about God. I had no intention of growing. God tried to speak to me through many ways—through people, messages, songs, etc. It says in the book of Job 33:14–17, *"For God speaks in one way and in two, though people do not perceive it. In a dream, in a vision of the night, when deep sleep falls on mortals, while they slumber on their beds, then he opens their ears, and terrifies them with warnings, that he may turn them aside from their deeds, and keep them from pride"*. But still I was nowhere close to listening to him.

Without realizing, I was slowly drifting away from God. I had become so bold that I had become rebellious and disobedient. I always thought what I did was right; I wouldn't let anyone win over an argument with me on anything. I did what I wanted to do; in the process I had to face many unpleasant consequences, but still in the midst of all that I could not bring myself not to pray. I could not sleep without praying no matter how tired I was, how late it was. I never believed in ritualistic prayer, which I was used to hearing at all times especially in my family, church, and gatherings, so I really did not want to pray how everybody-else prayed. I had come up with my own style of prayer. I basically thanked God for everything, told him what I wanted. Every promise that I read I believed. I meditated on my few favorite verses from the Bible, even though at that time all I read was the book of Psalms and Proverbs mainly at night. Then in the morning I just prayed without reading anything but again repeating my few favorite verses like, "I will instruct thee and teach thee in the way which thou shalt go" (Psalm 32:8), "The fear of the Lord is the beginning of the knowledge" (Proverbs 1:7), "By humility and the fear of the Lord are riches, honor and life" (Proverbs 22:4), "Pride goeth before destruction" (Proverbs 16:18), "and, lo, I am with you always, even unto the end of the world." (Matthew 28:20).

Every time I left the house to go somewhere, I would always say the prayer that one of my aunts, a very good family friend, had taught me when I was little; a simple but very effective prayer (which, by the way, I still say when I leave the house, and I would encourage everyone to do the same; it does make a difference especially when you believe what you say), i.e., "God be with me as I am going out now," even though the places at that time that I was going I knew were not the safest or right places to go. But maybe it was because of my innocent prayer or maybe because of my childlike faith in God that I always returned back home safe and sound.

Those days I was very skinny and looked like if someone had breathed on me I would just disappear. What I mean to say is I was not even physically strong and tough, but still people had some kind of fear. People would not dare to even speak foul language about me or around me, even if I was in the midst of wrong people at the wrong places at the wrong time. I still remember a sentence someone had said about me. "Hey, watch out your language. Look who is sitting with us," even though I never actually said a word to them. I used to hang out with people with whom you do not want to associate with if you are decent, but even then no matter what I did, people did not seem to mind being around me, which, of course, in turn encouraged me more because I knew that no matter what I do, people will like me anyway. Not that I did any favor to them, actually it was the other way around.

Now I understand that God's favor was upon me even though at that time I was miles away from him. Why? I still find it difficult to see any reason. That is what I refer to as "God's unconditional love"—the kind of love we cannot find anywhere in this world. He does not need to have a reason to love us except that he is the one who created us; it hurts him to see that his creation is drifting away from him trying to serve the wrong master. He knows exactly where it will take us and he makes every effort to stop us going in that direction.

I used to stay in a hostel or dorm, as you call here; many times I did not follow dorm rules, but did I ever get punished? No, because the warden/ supervisor of the hostel for some reason liked me in spite of all the wrong things that I did. She even brought food to me in my room if I missed dinner- time and practically begged me to eat. Often she used to threaten me saying that she will tell of my works to my brother, Babanna, who was also stay- ing there as kind of my guardian. She even did that a couple of times. Even though my brother would just lovingly ask me why I did what I did, still it would bring tears in my eyes that would not stop even long after he had left. It used to really make me feel sad thinking that it hurts him especially because I myself did not know why I did those things knowing fully well that they were not the right things. I do not think there is any word to describe such a person or such actions.

Then I joined nursing where again I had to stay in a dorm. Everybody treated me as if I was a very special person. For four years my friends brought breakfast for me in my room in bed as they knew I would not get up early enough and the breakfast time would be over. They did not want me to starve till lunch time. All of my classmates were from a southern state of India known as Kerala. They could not speak any other language other than their mother tongue, Malayalam, except for the three girls. Somehow they were able to communicate with me, because of which I think I survived, being the only non-Malayali girl among them. People used to call me, "English speaking Malayali."

Today, after twenty-five years plus, some of my best friends are from among those girls and we are still so close to each other. In addition to that, their children are friends of my children. My friends used to say about me "oru sadhanam" in Malayalam language, which meant "You are some-thing." One of my closest friends always used to say, "ninde katyavnnu ninde kondu madatu pova," which meant "Whoever marries you will get tired of you," or they will say "ninde kattiyonde kashta kaala,"which meant "Your husband's difficult time," and many things like that, to which I never paid attention or cared. But now when I think about my friends I feel bad that I never did any favor to them in return—I was always on the receiving end.

Somehow I finished my nursing and became a clinical instructor in Mysore, India. Even though initially everybody was a stranger to me there, still I received special treatment and favor from everyone.

Then I got married and came to the US. Even here, too, at my work, there was exception to my demands and needs, especially my supervisor in Henry Ford Hospital who met my every need, allowed flexible schedule, which of course had caused some conflicts between the other employees, but still that did not cause that supervisor to treat me any different. Even the job that I got at Henry Ford Hospital was something that I did not even deserve—the job practically fell on my lap without any effort. I had not even applied for that job as I did not have a nursing license then. I had just made a phone call to that hospital to inquire about the refresher course as someone had advised me to do so. They had said it might help me in passing the state board exam for nursing to get the nursing license but when I had asked them about the refresher course they connected me to the nursing supervisor on one of the nursing units, who after asking me some basic questions hired me immediately as a registered nurse. Then, of course, I had to fulfill the obligations of getting the license, which I did. Everything and everyone contributed in making me feel very proud of myself. I thought it was all because of me, because I was so good, intelligent, talented. How could you not feel proud of yourself when everybody else around you treated you that special way? People made me feel I was extraordinary, extra special, even though I was not. I did everything my way or no way. Nobody could convince me if I was doing anything wrong.

I had enjoyed life so much in a worldly way; the beautiful places we saw the time me and my husband spent together, it was just unbelievable. Even after we had kids, we enjoyed with them so much but slowly I realized these moments of happiness just lasted for sometime. Each time, something that I enjoyed was only for that moment then I forgot about it then I wanted more—a different kind of experience, a different adventure to give me that happiness—until I reached a point when there was nothing else to explore nothing new to try, nothing exciting anymore, even though those moments of happiness I never really remembered. I could not even recall what had made me so happy—the things, the beautiful places that we saw did not seem to matter. How could you call that as happiness when the things that you enjoyed so much, you cannot even remember or recall? If I was really happy then, I would have easily remembered, right? Everything seemed to be vanity. There was not any excitement any more. I was looking for something, something of which I had no clue, something meaningful, something that will last, something I knew I had to find out—but what?

The things that I thought I had enjoyed, the happiness that I thought I had because of those things began to fade, especially when I realized my kids were growing up. I knew that they had not experienced the love of God in their lives as I did at their age and I thought if I continued to live like this then they will never experience God. So then slowly I tried to seek, look for happiness that would last, which, of course, I had it all along but I had not realized as I was running after the wrong things. I did not think that everything was vanity because I was trying to serve the wrong master. Finally I understood what vanity means in the book of Ecclesiastes, but it took me forty-plus years to realize that. It was God's grace that he had given me that many years in my life to at-least finally know what real happiness is, but would he give everyone this much life and opportunity to find that out? We will never know. Maybe that is why God wanted me to write this book—so people would come to know and understand what vanity is before it is too late.

I, now, always pray to God, "Please make my children know and choose to do your will now only so that they can use their lives to please and live for you." Even though I had accepted God at a very young age, still I did not know and choose to do the will of God until now, as it took a long time for me to listen to his voice, rather to confirm his voice. Maybe partly because after I had known about God, I was not in the right environment where I could grow as a Christian, or maybe he wanted me to wait, but now that I know I often question him, "Why did you not discipline me before?" And I question myself, "Why did I not listen before?" Why did I waste these many years of my life not doing his work?" But when I think about that, I understand that it was my pride that had stopped me from listening. It was then that God showed me the life of Moses. Why did God train him for eighty years before he used him for his work? God made sure Moses became humble enough in God's sight before he could use him. Even though he was the greatest leader, he still could not enter the promised land, so I did not want to be like Moses.

It takes a long time to admit we have pride in us. It is a sin that we commit that we do not even realize we are committing—a sin—and to come out of it we simply need God's grace; there is no other way to come out of it. I regret deeply now for wasting so many years of my life not doing what I am doing or trying to do, because the joy and happiness that I have now I did not get doing anything else in this world, not even watching the beautiful Niagara Falls, which is one of my favorite places. But ever since I have experienced God's love in my life, these have lasting memories. I never used to remember or recall what they looked like once I left those places, but now I can because now I see wonders of God in those sights. People say it is a natural wonder, but I say it is God's wonder—yet another one of the many reasons to adore and worship that great, amazing God. I had written a song, the lyrics of which goes like,

> God, your creation is so beautiful and
>     amazing
> Yet you have transformed a sinner like me
>     in your image
> How can I ever thank you, God?

Even man has created many things which are named as "man-made wonders," which are beyond understanding for people like me who cannot even think how they did them even if there is full, detailed, extensive explanation. God certainly has given a wonder brain to some of those people who have come with man-made wonders like the Golden Gate Bridge, Eiffel Tower, Taj Mahal, the

Great Wall of China, etc., even the roads that we use every day. I always question, "How did they do it?" I wonder how many of those geniuses have acknowledged or given credit to the One, who has given them the brain to create something like that. But whosoever have built them must have been awfully proud of themselves, don't you think?

I am assuming people who have experienced God would have given credit to God and glorified him. I would really like to read the history of those people who have created those man-made wonders someday, as I like to know how many of them actually felt proud of themselves. Did they eventually experience vanity? There always comes a point in our lives when everything is going good and great for us and we are in a position when everything we touch becomes gold, we tend to become proud. What I mean to say is that when we are so prosperous and wealthy in life, pride easily makes a way into our lives, knowingly or unknowingly. Of course in the beginning we may not even realize until it is too late. Don't get me wrong, even people who are poor and have nothing in terms of knowledge, talents, wealth etc., still can harbor pride in their lives. Satan is very subtle in handling us in those kinds of situations. He makes us feel nothing is wrong by doing something, until it is too late when we find out that everything is wrong.

Of course then we are the one who have to pay the price with whatever we have, whatever may be the cost. Sometimes God will give us a chance to come back, repent, and sometimes he will say it is too late. In either case, we are at risk, so if anyone is reading this book I would advise you it is not worth taking that risk no matter how adventurous you are as a human being.

See, when pride made a way in my life, I did not really have anything that extraordinary to boast about—no talents, no riches, no intelligence, not even a loving heart—but because I trusted in God so much in spite of everything that I did, I think I just found favor with people, which made me feel proud of myself. The worst part was that I was happy with that feeling and did not think anything was wrong feeling that way. It did not really matter whether I did right or wrong, people wouldn't condemn me. They were willing to do things for me that I did not deserve at all. Everything came to me easy; opportunities just knocked on my door without any of my effort, because of which I did not value them.

I wanted to become somewhat like King David in the Bible, who from being a shepherd boy rose up to be a king of Israel all because God was pleased with him. Even though many times he did things that he knew were wrong, yet God forgave him each time. I had thought of that a lot: How can somebody do things like David did, yet when he went in God's presence he could please God? What was so different about David that other people in the Bible did not have? After pondering a lot, finally I came to a conclusion that I think David had a child's heart. In fact he was always a child; he never grew up even after he became a king. He was a very impulsive person yet when it came to God he had love, fear, reverence, and was willing to wait. Even though he did things he knew were wrong, he never hesitated to humble himself enough before God to acknowledge and repent of his mistakes.In fact I think he never had pride in his heart at any time. See, pride comes when people grow up.

Children do not have pride in their hearts or lives. They are not afraid or intimidated to ask someone else if they do not know something, they do not think twice to say sorry to someone even if it was not their mistake, they are able to forgive and forget easily, and many characteristics like that which our God wants in us when we become his children. He says the kingdom of heaven belongs to little children. Luke 18:16–17 says, "Let the little children come to me, and do not stop them; for it is to such as these that the kingdom of God belongs."

I recall the way he (David) prayed to God for the people even after becoming a king; that is mentioned in the book of Chronicles. I loved the sincerity, his concern, and love for his people; it was so touching the way he pleads. 1 Chronicles 21:17 says, "And David said unto God, Is it not I that commanded the people to be numbered? even I it is that have sinned and done evil indeed; but as for these sheep, what have they done? let thine hand, I pray thee, O Lord my God, be on me, and on my father's house; but not on thy people, that they should be plagued."

It was a prayer of a child who admits wholeheartedly his mistakes and wants the best for other people. I do not think any adult can pray like that. It is difficult for me to think if he had a forgiving spirit, but he certainly had the concern for other people. He knew that there is no place on earth or in heaven that he can hide himself, but he was a human like us—he had doubts, fears, love, emotions, desires that he could not control. Yet he knew one thing—that his God is above all. He was not ashamed to go to him for anything and everything—he always poured out his heart to him. Good or bad, he confessed everything and repented never to repeat those mistakes again. He accepted God's decision for his life without questioning. He seemed to understand God's ways little. He knew

God is righteous and just; as such he knew even though God will forgive him when he repents, still he will punish him for the wrong he has done, and even that he accepts gracefully. David was forgiven of his sins but that did not stop him from facing the consequences because of his sins, which was about the adulterous act of him with the beautiful woman, Bathsheba, resulting in the death of his child (2 Samuel, chapters 11 and 12).

Scriptures are given to us so that we do not make the same mistakes but rather learn from our ancestors who had made those mistakes so we could be wiser. But do we do that, especially grown-up people in whom pride has already built a big, strong nest? Pride stops us from listening. So I urge you, do not fall prey to this pride, which can destroy your life knowingly or unknowingly. But instead become like little children who will be willing to listen and wise enough to stay away from pride that God hates.

I think God was waiting for me to make the choice to choose to serve only him, after which my life changed completely and I was transformed into a person whom he wanted me to be. It did not matter any more what people thought or would think of me. All I wanted to do was what God wanted me to do. It became my first priority to please my God, to obey every word that he spoke. All of a sudden it became very important to me that God should give my testimony. I wanted him to give me a "certificate of excellence" for my life. Little did I know the problems that I would encounter because of that decision living in this world. It is not easy to live a life like that, and it says very clearly in the word of God, "People will hate you because they hated me." John 15:18 says, "If the world hate you, ye know that it hated me before it hated you." But since I had not read the whole Bible, I was not aware of those difficulties that I was going to face in the days to come. My only desire was to please God at any cost. I wanted my life to be a living testimony for God. I wanted to serve only one master once I realized everything else in this world is vanity.

God is constantly using his surveillance camera to look for people who will be willing to give what he asks and do what he says.

# Salvation Is Free but the Rest Needs to Be Paid

Man is always looking for happiness and joy that is lasting which I found in God, but then it again comes with a price tag. Salvation is free, it is God's grace, but the rest needs to be paid. It was a huge price that Jesus had paid for sinners like us by dying on the cross for our sins so that whoever believes in him can have eternal, happier, everlasting life. To get the happiness that God will give, he asks us to be obedient to his every commandment, to be crucified with him, buried with him, and resurrect with him. Are we willing to do that—which is called baptism? Which is again a very controversial subject, but I am not interested in arguing about that. Instead, I just want you to know that it is referred to as the second birth and every one needs to be born again to see the kingdom of God, as John 3:3 says in the Scriptures, "Except a man be born again, he cannot see the kingdom of God."

Once we are dead, for this world means when we are resurrected we have to be a new creature. Do you think that will be easy? Especially when you have to live with the same old people after your resurrection, that is if you do make that choice. It is very difficult to live then because now the people whom you are going to live with are not new creatures, so when you are transformed in a new person it is very difficult for the other people to accept the "new" you, and that can create conflicts. Then how do we live or how can we have the happiness that God is promising? God's definition of happiness is different from ours. He says we will be joyful and happy in all circumstances even in pain and suffering. How can that be possible? But believe me—it is possible. You might think I am crazy—it does not make any sense. And you are right—it does not make any sense for people who have not experienced that resurrection power. When you do, it will make perfect sense. Then you will know and understand exactly what I am talking about.

It is natural to ask then, How can you be happy when you are having all kinds of problems in life or someone you love the most is suffering? That is the mystery of God's love which you just have to experience to know for yourself. I can say this with confidence because I have experienced that peace and joy during my suffering; it is not just me who has experienced that but there are many who I am sure can bear witness to that. It is an open invitation to all regardless of age, sex, creed, etc.—the only requirement is that you should be willing to believe and accept Jesus Christ as your savior who came for you, died for you, resurrected, and now sits at the right hand of the Father interceding on your behalf to give the happiness, love, joy, and peace that he has promised. Not that you do not feel the pain, but your pain is shared with the Almighty God who will eventually lift you up in ways you will never know, imagine, or understand. He may not do the way you want him to do, but he will do what is best for you, which you may or may not understand. He will give you the strength to endure and overcome.

There can be several reasons for God to put us in those situations; I will just give some. One may be that he is reproving you of something that you may not know about, or it could be that someone else can learn a lesson from your experience, or maybe God wants to bring someone that he has chosen for his works closer to him, or maybe God is preparing you to do something for him, etc. Overall purpose is to glorify him because that is the sole purpose that we are created in the beginning—to please God. It says, "for thou hast created all things, and for thy pleasure they are and were created." (Revelation 4:11).

One day one of our church members, Sanjay, was sharing his testimony of doing what he called a "dangerous prayer," which, of course, reminded me of my teenage years when I had worded the same for the prayer that I had prayed when I took my first step toward God. I was very young and innocent at that time, with many unanswered questions of life itself, except one thing that I was so sure about—that Jesus is God. I had said then, "God, if I ever go away from you, then do something that can make me come back to you; do not ever make me so comfortable in life that I can forget about you." Even though I prayed like that, God never really made me suffer for anything maybe because of so much faith that I had in me, or maybe because of my innocence or unawareness of God's expectations from me, or maybe it was just his grace, I do not know!

One Sunday, the message by our pastor's brother about King Uzziah in the Old Testament of Scriptures mimicked my lifestyle, the way I was living, and it brought back the memory of the pride that I had which I was refusing to acknowledge or accept. God had prospered King Uzziah as long as he sought the Lord, had his fear, and he did what was right in the sight of God; but the minute he let pride enter in him, it led him to destruction. You can read his story in the second book of Chronicles.

Chapter 26 verses 4–5 says, *"He did what was right in the sight of the Lord, just as his father Amaziah had done. He set himself to seek God in the days of Zechariah, who instructed him in the fear of God; and as long as he sought the Lord, God made him prosper."* And then from verses 15–16, it says, *"And his fame spread far, for he was marvelously helped until he became strong. But when he had become strong, he grew proud, to his destruction. For he was false to the Lord his God."* Then of course it goes on to say he became disobedient, refusing to listen, finally making God angry. The Lord punishes King Uzziah by striking him with leprosy and he eventually dies as a leprous man. Verse 21 says, "And Uz-zi-ah the king was a leper unto the day of his death and dwelt in a several house, being a leper; for he was cut off from the house of the Lord:" What a sad story to happen for a king whom God had blessed so much all because of one thing—pride—which as you have noticed led to other sins that God does not appreciate.

Something like that happened to me too. It did not matter how many wrong things I did, God kept on giving me opportunities, messages, to turn back to him, which I obviously ignored. Many times I knew he was trying to warn me but since I was not hearing the voices as I hear now, it was difficult for me to listen. Those were the times I even used to ask forgiveness for the things that I did wrong but then again I would do something else wrong, sometimes even knowingly, but even then God did not turn his face away from me.

But when I let pride come in me, I could not even ask for forgiveness because then everything that I was doing seemed right to me and so I did not even realize when I lost God's presence in my life. Satan is so subtle. It says in 1 Peter 5:8, "Be sober, be vigilant; because your adversary the devil, as a roaring lion, walketh about, seeking whom he may devour:_" If I had realized, maybe I would have said sorry, but it took twenty-plus years to know that I had lost his presence and accept that I was wrong. Please do not ever underestimate the power of Satan. He even tried to devour Jesus—who was and is the Son of God. The good news is that Jesus defeated his advances, won the victory for us. So the only way we can now defeat Satan is through Jesus. Through him alone we can become victorious.

There is a proverb, "Beauty lies in the eyes of the beholder," which is very true. What may look beautiful to you may not look beautiful to another person. A lot of times, especially in marriages, when someone does not turn out to meet our expectations, we find ourselves saying, "How in the world so and so got married to such a person?" or we say, "He or she is not even good-looking or even otherwise," and we come with a statement, "So and so does not deserve such a person." But it is the person who is married to that person who really knows the reason, who understands whether it is good or not. We are so quick to pass judgment on others. There is something beautiful in every person which only the person in love can see and feel. A lot of times people say people who are beautiful to look at are not really good at heart, which is also not true. We cannot just generalize like that based on somebody's experience because the external beauty does not last long until and unless there is something beautiful internally. The relationship does not last until there is some kind of divine intervention. A person can only become beautiful in every aspect when God intervenes, when his love is in that person. A person has to have God living in him or her to become the most beautiful person in this world. Then only the beauty will be seen by everyone who comes across that person.

If you do not have God living in you, then the beauty can invite pride in your heart again, which is the root cause of all the problems. Again and again throughout the Bible, we are told *pride leads to destruction* and advises us to be humble. As such, I will be very happy, if and, when God will testify of me by saying, "This is my daughter who is humble enough to belong to me"—that will be the happiest day of my life and probably the last day of my life on this earth when God will take me away from this world to be with him, when I fulfill his will and purpose of my life and when God will say he is pleased with me.

I know that will surely happen because it is his promise that says, "Behold, I stand at the door, and knock: if any man hear my voice, and open the door, I will come into him and will sup with him, and he with me." (Revelation 3:20). I have opened the door for him to come in since long back. Even though he has entered in, yet many times I feel he has not dined with me. As I know, for God to dine with me or in other words to dwell in me, I have to meet his standards. I have to live a life that is pleasing to him, love him with all my heart,mind and soul, obey his every commandment. I cannot pick and choose what I want or like. I have to give up my will to his will. I have to keep myself holy and to do all that it might take a lifetime; still I have the desire to strive for that because I know it is worth it. Nothing else will give me more joy than this for which I need God's grace. We will never know when we will be meeting his standards, not until he reveals to us.

At first I thought the Bible or the Scriptures is all that we have. If we obey and follow exactly what the Bible says, that is it; but then I found out there is more to it than what is written in the Scriptures. God tells us more, explains to us more, makes us understand more, but we need listening ears for that and an obedient heart. The Scriptures are written by people who are inspired by the Holy Spirit to whom God spoke, and they recorded, but that does not mean he has stopped talking to people 2,000 years back. He still talks; we do not record, we do not hear, or we do not want to hear because then we feel we are obligated to do what we hear, which we may or may not like, especially if it does not agree with our logic and understanding. That means we have to give up something that belongs to us though we do not really realize that "something" is given to us by God himself. Still we are reluctant to give back to God what really belongs to him in the first place.

But there were people who had done that in the past and have received God's blessings, especially the one who is mentioned in the Bible, Abraham, who is a perfect example in the book of Genesis chapters 12–25 (you can read his story there). I often wonder if I will ever have the faith of Abraham. In one instance, God asks him to leave his comfort zone, where he was well settled, and go to a place that he was going to show as he would go. Can you picture that? If I was Abraham, I would have asked

God hundreds of question: God, at least give me the name of the place that I am going before I start my journey. What will my wife say? What will my folks think of me? etc. At least I should have some answers to give them if not for me. But Abraham did not ask even one question. As it says, "he did what the Lord has told him to do."

Then in another instance, we see that God had yet given Abraham another promise—promise of a child in the most unlikely situation. Yet God had made him wait for so many years to fulfill that promise—twenty-five years. And then after he fulfills that promise of a promised child, Isaac, after making him wait for those long twenty-five years, God tells him to give him back what he himself had given out of his free will. What is more interesting is that even then, Abraham does exactly what the Lord tells him without asking a single question or expressing his concerns. I even give lot of credit to his son Isaac, who obeys his father even though I think by then, he was a teenager. Can you imagine children of this generation doing that? But then the parents these days are not even close to Abraham. What I did not understand was why would God do something like that? But then I read that story multiple times; it says in Genesis 22:12, "Now I know that you fear God." I was puzzled to read that. I had to read that a couple of times because all this time I thought God knows everything about a human being. So I thought, *How could God not know whether Abraham feared him or not?* But, the more I thought I felt, God knows everything about a human being except what choice the human will make, as God has given human beings the freedom to make a choice. But then I felt that cannot be right either, so I had asked this question to one preacher that I had met recently. What he explained was something that did make sense to me as he gave some Bible references. He said God knows everything before the foundation of this earth, and in this case, he was just approving or attesting what Abraham had done, maybe to increase his faith or for his encouragement. Maybe that is why he puts us through certain trials and situations—to find out if we will do what he expects or wants us to do, not for God to know, but rather, for us to know the approval of God, which would make us more confident and stand firm in our faith.

Abraham had passed that test, but will we? God does not want us to pay back what he had paid for us because we will never be able to do that even if we wanted to, but he asks us to do very simple things like to have faith, to do what he tells us to do without questioning, to love him, etc. So it is a very small price he is asking us to pay in return to what he has done, and he is still willing to do more for us. As such, God is constantly using his surveillance camera to look for people who will be willing to give what he asks and do what he says; in other words, get rid of our pride which stops us from listening and be obedient, but know that knowing his will calls for accountability.

# Knowing His Will Calls for Accountability

This is something I had been told very clearly, that I have to share my thoughts on this in my church, but every time I decided I would, something would happen and I was unable to do so. Then I asked God why he always does that to me—why he makes me wait to share something that I know for sure that he wants me to share—sometimes it is answers to my prayers and sometimes revelations. I always feel as if people in my church never have any problem sharing what the Lord does for them, but then why do I have a problem? I just feel if I have to do something anyway, why not just do it and get it over with? But God does not let us do it that way. He does not want us to do something just for the sake of doing it. He wants us to do it with all our heart, sometimes wants us to try to understand his ways, his timings, and the things he wants to reveal to us—his will, his desire, and his purpose. Most of the questions that I ask God—he answers them in different ways.

I was almost about to publish this book but still something was stopping, and now I know why and what, about which I am writing here. One weekend in our church we had special prayer meetings. A special speaker, Noble Thomas, was invited. I was not motivated enough to attend these meetings; as such I decided not to go that Friday night. But my husband, after attending that meeting, told me that it was really good, and that many people were blessed by that meeting. Even then I didn't have any desire to attend the following day. I was scheduled to work that Saturday so I prayed, "God, if you really want me to go to that meeting, then give me a day off." As often happens with me, I got a day off so I had no excuse for not going to that meeting.

Nothing special happened in that meeting; the message, of course, was very nice, but it was something that I had written long back for one of my other book. For some reason I felt sad thinking that I will be missing next day Sunday service as I was scheduled to work, but then our pastor suddenly announced there will be evening service on Sunday, which we never usually have. It made me very happy. It was as if God was reading my mind, which made our pastor arrange that special service for me.

So after work I attended the Sunday evening meeting where God gave me something to write again. It's amazing how smoothly God arranges everything we want or need. He gave me one more new song to write before the message began and then the message was about Apostle Paul, when God had revealed him about the third heaven. He said it took fourteen years for Paul to reveal it to people. I don't know if he had experienced what I had experienced—pride—which I doubt if he did, being the great apostle that he was.

As when we know some secrets, we are dying to tell somebody, but Paul had kept that secret for so many years. How could one do that? As when God reveals to me something, I want to tell the whole world everything. You know why? Because of pride that comes in me, even though I know it is not because of any of my efforts that I come to know the secrets of God. It is God who chooses to reveal certain secrets to certain people—maybe one of which is me. I know very well it is all because of his grace and favor that he reveals to me, but still I am tempted to take credit for that—you can call it a spiritual pride—it is then that God stops me from doing or sharing something.

One Sunday, one of our church members, Rani, had shared her testimony about her car—how God took care of her problem when she prayed about it, trusted enough in God to handle the problem. It was very touching. Then she said she was not sure whether she should share this small incident in church as she felt she might waste time in church. But I think testimonies are never a waste of time because whoever shares those are sharing their personal experiences with God coming straight from their hearts out of gratitude, and whenever or wherever God is involved, it is never a waste of time. It touches people's hearts, encourages them because it is possible that someone could be in that same situation and God is trying to reach out to that person through those testimonies. God himself says to tell of his works among people so his name will be glorified (Psalm 96:3). It does not specify whether what we share is what we consider a small or big testimony. God's wondrous works are wondrous no matter what they are—how big or small they may be—so we have to testify no matter what to glorify his name. We do not have to be in a life-and-death situation to tell of his works because every breath that we take itself is a miracle—something that we should be able to testify to glorify and offer sacrifices of praise and thanskgiving to him.

Many times suddenly I get thoughts that I never think about. I know then those thoughts cannot be mine, but since I do not always hear the audible voice, I wait to confirm before I share with people. But for me I always have to write them down, otherwise I forget what I hear. When God gives thoughts, he also tells when and where to share those thoughts. Often I plan to share my thoughts in our prayer meetings thinking it will be a smaller group, but somehow my lips get sealed for some reason; eventually I end up sharing them in church. Then when some people (many times those people I do not even know) come and tell me that they really needed to hear what I had shared, then I understand why I was not able to share in those meetings. If we want to please God, then we have to do exactly the way he tells us to do even if we are tempted to do differently. Even though many times it may not seem anything is wrong with that little deviation to us, but it can be considered disobedience in God's sight.

I have experienced the consequences of doing such things, so now I make sure I do not change anything when I am prompted by God to do something even if it does not make any sense to me. I try to do exactly the way he tells me to do something, but sometimes it is not easy especially if we have to depend on others to do something. As then we are obligated to explain to them why we are doing something the way we are doing, which they may or may not understand. I do not try to analyze anymore when I am told to do something; now I say, "God, I am willing to do what you want me to do, but you have to provide opportunity for me, make a way for what you want me to do." And believe it or not, he does make a way when and where I feel there is no way.

One Wednesday, during prayer meeting at someone's house, everything that I wanted to share was spoken by our guest pastor who had come from India. For some time now, at least a couple of people in our church had expressed their desire to do something for God and the church that I go to, which had really touched me. I was personally very happy as it was one of my desires and in my prayer list that everyone in our church will have the desire to serve God, this church. But as our pastor says, it is good to wait until God reveals what exactly we have to do. I think it is good in a way because then you will have time to prepare yourselves to hear what God says for you to do. Because what he wants you to do might be the things that you may not be expecting, which maybe difficult for you to do but once he tells you, he will expect you to do those no matter what. Then you cannot pick and choose or even refuse to do something that he tells you, especially if you want to be obedient to him.

There is a word of caution in Ecclesiastes 5:5. It says, "It is better that you should not vow than that you should vow and not fulfill it," and also verse 4 says, "When you make a vow to God, do not delay in fulfilling it". I wish someone had told me this before I got myself in this situation as I am still struggling to do what God has asked me to do. Maybe not everybody is as difficult as me for him to deal with, because I do not yield easily, which I know is not good. I question, I argue, I refuse, yet I know he wants to use me, and he does—I just do not understand. It reminds me of Jonah in the Old Testament in Scriptures, who had received very clear instructions from God what he wants him to do, yet Jonah tried to do his own way and ended up causing trouble for himself and others. So he is one character whom I really do not like as it always makes me feel guilty when I do not do what I know I have to do.

Many times pride comes in my way of doing because I feel I know better and think I can do better. I don't feel anything wrong doing my way little deviation from what God tells me to do, even though now I know it is totally wrong, yet I try to compromise, make a deal with him, giving my excuses and explanations. My rationale is it should not matter as long as I am doing what I am told, but you could be one of the people like Moses who could not reach the promised land because of that little deviation, distrust or Pride (Numbers 20:1–13). Of course now I don't do that anymore. I have lost too many blessings because of my ways, my pride.

Anyway, just after my water baptism about little over three years back, when I was struggling with everything else, I was hearing voices telling me what to do, revealing things that I never imagined or even wanted to know. I had enough problems of my own to deal with at that time and God was telling me to do something for others. Every time I tried to pray for myself, my family, I was told to pray for somebody else, and that, too, for somebody who I hardly knew or cared for. It was so frustrating but slowly I understood what God wanted me to do, i.e., he wanted me to start caring for others as I do for myself, which I never did before; I mean, I used to care but only about people I liked to care about, that too only after I took care of me and my family first. I was so proud of myself and my family.

I always thought charity begins at home but I was wrong. I am not saying we should neglect ourselves or our family either. Let me see if I can explain this little bit better by this example. Say someone in your neighborhood is dying but someone whom you love very much is sick at home;

who you will choose to help first? Many of you might immediately answer help the dying person first, right? But for me, before I came to Christ, my answer would have been I would help first the person I love most who is sick at home, but now my answer is different—I would help the dying person first. Hope I am getting the message across right. See, God has changed my mentality, about caring for others. So once I started praying sincerely for other people's needs, God took care of my needs, my problems at home. It was then I remembered what the Lord did for Job in the Bible when he prayed for his friends (Job 42:10).

If we want blessings then we need to bless others. We need to sincerely care and pray for others, to think of their problems as our own, their happiness as our own. We have to give up something that we are holding so tight to hear what God has to say to us. He wants us to separate ourselves from what means so much to us so that he can do his work through us. It can be anything that we are attached to—maybe our material things or job or our loved ones, spouse, children, etc. He wants us to come all alone to him, forsaking everything, then only we will hear him speak to us. God wants us to put him first above everything else. He does not necessarily want us to give something but just wants us to know that we are willing to give any-

or everything to him without thinking twice. Like Abraham, who was ready to give up his promised child, Isaac, only then did God provide Abraham what he needed for sacrifice at that point. I think we should all try to find out what we are holding so tight that is a barrier between us and God. For me, it was pride, but I thought it was my son Vince, but God had used him to make me admit what I was refusing to admit. Once I knew and accepted that my pride was the barrier and then let go of it, I felt myself closer to God, and then I started to hear from him. Then I started telling him that I wanted to do something for him.

I was trying to figure out what I am good at. The only thing that I felt I was really good at was painting, so I thought maybe God will make use of that talent for his glory. But when I asked God, what he told me was completely different, certainly not what I had expected. He told me to do certain things which I never did before, which I felt I was not capable of doing, of which one was to sing, which I am still struggling to do. The reason is that I never sang in my life before. The only time I remember when I sang was for my tenth-grade exams as it was mandatory. And then the second time I had to sing was a Malayalam song in college, again it was something I had to do. So I was very sure that God knew that I do not sing and do not like to sing, at least not in front of people, yet he had asked me to do that. So then, of course, I questioned, argued, and asked God if he really knows what he is asking me to do, hoping he will change his mind and tell me to do something else instead, but when God says something it is final; he seldom changes it, it is up to us to obey or not.

A couple of years back, Dr. Clifford Kumar, a great servant of God who is also related to me through my husband, came to our house during his mission tour to the US. He had a long talk with me when I had just asked him casually one simple question, i.e., how he writes songs, as he had written so many songs. But as he started to tell me, I wished at that time maybe I should not have asked him anything at all, as the conversation that followed made me feel very guilty. Then he sang one song which started to haunt me daily, reminding me of my vow that I made to God. During one Sunday service, our pastor had talked about the fig tree parable in Luke 13:6–9. It was about the tree that was there for three years without bearing any fruit. When the owner comes and sees that, he says to the gardener to cut the tree down as it was not bearing any fruit, but somehow the gardener convinces the owner that he will take care of it for another year; and if it still does not bear fruit next year, then he will cut it down. Suddenly it opened my eyes to see what God was trying to tell me, that is, what will happen to me if I did not do what he had asked me to do? It was as if Jesus was the gardener interceding on my behalf to God, who was the owner. See, Jesus always talked in parables to make us understand better.

It is amazing how God talks to you through different ways, makes us do things that we are reluctant to do. So once I got the message, I made up my mind and sang on New Year's Eve. After that incidence, I made a decision to bear fruit for him and be a fruitful tree. I do not want my Jesus to be ashamed of me. He died for me and here I am refusing to do a simple thing for him.

The reason I am sharing all this is so that you can be ready for whatever God asks you to do. He might ask anything for you to do, not just what you are good at. It might even be very difficult especially if it is something that you have never done before in your life, which is beyond your abilities and talents. Like that example of Zechariah from the Levites, even though he might have been better as a priest, since he came from a Levite family, God used him as a prophet.

The song which my uncle, Dr. Clifford Kumar sang in Hindi, was "Gaane ka dil aur bajaane ka jeevan," which meant "Everyone has been given a heart to sing and play music," is the one that taught me to write songs. Of course the rest of the lyrics of that song reflects my life. How simple it is to receive his choicest blessings, we just have to invite Jesus in our lives. So, anyway, once I surrendered my will to his will, he blessed me with all the blessings that I felt I did not even deserve. He did not make anything any easier for me either, in fact every blessing that I received was as if I had to fight for it through God who said, "The battle belongs to me" (1 Samuel 17:47). But the condition was that I should not lose faith in him, which seemed so difficult at times when things seemed to be going exactly in the opposite direction in my view, especially with all the proofs that I had pointing in that direction. That was the time when God had started giving me songs to write, so you can imagine my frustration. Here nothing was happening according to his promises to me; on top of that he was asking me to do something that I did not know how to do. But thanks to his grace I was able to do both, i.e., to keep faith and write songs. The very first song that I wrote, which I am sharing here, is the one that I literally heard driving on my way to work one day. I will translate in English as I had written this song in Hindi. It is not easy to translate word by word, but I'll try to keep the lyrics as close as possible:

My Jesus, my Jesus,
My Jesus, you're the creator
My Jesus, you're the one who gives salvation
My Jesus, you're the one who sustains
My Jesus, my Jesus

You make my heart to be yours
and make me live for you
Let me to get transformed in you
so that I can see with my eyes
all your glorious works

You teach me how to have faith
and also how to stand firm in faith
Do not let Satan touch us
My Jesus, you see to it from heaven
so that your promises can come true
in my life

You are the light of my heart
You stay in my heart always
Let never darkness make room
Let there be only light in my heart
Let all the people see your light
from my life

Someone rightfully has said, "God does not always choose the qualified but he qualifies those he chooses." I did not know the ABCDs of how to write songs or make tunes, yet I have written several songs during the trial I was going through. I have not made them public yet as I am still working on those. Anyway, so be ready for whatever God tells you to do. It may be something that you never did in your life before or something you know how to do, but either way do not neglect doing what he tells you to do. You can face serious consequences if you do not. Just remember always—knowing his will calls for accountability.

I was wondering...what is so great, so special in the name of Jesus—who most people do not even acknowledge as God—that when we accept and believe in him can change a person, their whole personality, their life?

# What Is So Special in the Name of Jesus?

I remember a famous couple, Shoury Babu and his wife, who were once a famous karate champion and a classical Indian dancer. I came to know (them) firsthand through one of our mutual friends. Who would think people like them can be lonely? They had everything—health, wealth, and fame—but still there was some emptiness in their lives, a desire to seek something, something unknown which they did not have to satisfy them. So, at the peak of their career they searched for God and found him, which eventually changed their lives. From that time onward there was no turning back for them, they had willingly left everything, followed Jesus, and now doing full-time ministry as per their testimony.

They are not the only ones but there are many like them who have given up everything they owned to do the will of God once they had a personal encounter with Jesus. That can only happen when pride is not in a person as only then can a person be humble enough to look beyond himself, within himself, and get the desire or wisdom to seek God—Jesus. I was wondering what makes people do that. What is so great, so special in the name of Jesus—who most people do not even acknowledge as God—that when we accept and believe in him, can change a person, their whole personality, their life? Then they will be willing to sacrifice anything and everything that rightfully belongs to them and do what Jesus tells them to do. They are willing to carry the cross and suffer for his name's sake. Why? Why would anybody leave all the luxurious things of this world and the comfortable lifestyle just to please Jesus? Does any of this make sense? I think many people will label these people as "crazy people" or "foolish people." But from what I have experienced now, I can understand and say that they are the wisest people, for they have made the wisest decision in their lives.

People who say there is no God—can they explain this mystery? I bet they cannot, because this is something you have to experience to understand. No one will be able to explain to them either, not even the greatest and best preacher in the world, unless and until the Lord himself chooses to do so. Like it says in the book of Ecclesiastes, no human can even figure out the beginning or the end of what God did and what God will do. But I can say without doubt that these are the wisest, happiest people on earth because what these people experience is heavenly—a joy and peace that no man can give or take away, for which they are willing to trade any earthly comfort that they have.

I sometimes watch the *Discovery Channel* on television with my husband. Most of the time he goes to sleep while I end up watching the entire program. Once when I was watching, I was amazed at people trying to find the evidence about whether the Bible indeed was true or whether Jesus indeed existed on this earth. They are trying to find clues and proof for that, but I am sure even if they spend their lifetime trying to find those they will never find. Maybe they will be able to find little odds and ends because they fail to understand that God has given only a fraction of his brain to humans, and it is his promise that he will never ever give more wisdom to any human being after King Solomon.

And if that king, the wisest person on earth, has said that, we will never know what God does; it is just foolishness, waste of time, energy, and resources to prove something that they will never be able to prove. What I do not understand is that why people have to go through all that trouble, all they need to do is seek God and they will find the evidence right there. Why make things compli-cated and also make everyone else confused? Again it is the choice one has to make. God has given that privilege to people to choose. Do we want to choose to believe in him or not? If we do, then we will be relieved of all the tension, stress, and frustration trying to find something that is already there, but if we do not then we will be frustrated throughout our life trying to find something that we will never find. Makes sense, right?

If we ask God, he can easily reveal to us things provided we meet his standards because when he created human beings, it was to talk to us, hear from us, have fellowship with us, but then iniquity came which separated us from him; as such we could no longer do that. But still God wants to have and restore that relationship with us without having to destroy any soul. That is why he has put a mediator between him and us—Jesus—who intercedes for us on our behalf, trying to reconcile everyone with him. But people who are hardhearted—proud of themselves—cannot cross that barrier because pride is something that is mentioned in the Bible, which says it leads us to destruction. What more can happen after that? Pride stops people from listening, and when we stop listening we stop everything else in our lives. I cannot think of anyone who was proud and still lived a happy life. I am sure that person has eventually experienced the destruction caused by pride. It is God's word that says in Proverbs 30:5, "Every word of God's proves true."

Pride takes away the peace that God wants to give and can give in the midst of our adversaries. We cannot reach out to God even if we want to when we give room for pride. It had happened to me. I know what I went through and I certainly do not want anybody else going through what I did. It is painful, irreparable, ugly, and if you can avoid then I would advise you to do that—that is, of course, if you have not yet reached the point of not listening.

Our pastor, Reverend Rajan George, always quotes, "You can take the horse to the water but you cannot make him drink the water." The horse has to open his mouth to drink the water by itself. Same thing with people who are filled with pride; we can tell them all we want but until they realize they are under the influence of pride they will not listen. It is like pouring water on a pot which is kept upside down. The pot does not get filled with water but just pours out. The only person that can make them drink that water, or in other words make them realize, is God. But how can he do that when we are not ready to make that choice?

See, one of the problems of God is that no matter what we do, he does not want to take away the freedom to choose from us, which he has given to us as human beings when he first created us. He is willing to forgive and forget every sin of ours provided we show even one sign that we are willing to make the choice to turn toward him. If we do that, then everything in our life is history, and we will start a new life with a clean slate. If we just take one step to come closer to him, we will see that he will take many steps to take us under his wings. Isn't that something worth a try? But would that *pride* let us go off that easy? No, I do not think so. It will be a tough fight, and those who win will be able to understand why this famous couple, and many others like them, did what they did, i.e., left everything for Jesus! If you ask them, "Was it worth it?" I am sure without thinking twice they will say, "Yes, it was well worth it," because of one simple reason. It is said in Matthew 6:33, "Seek ye first the kingdom of God and his righteousness and all these things shall be added unto you."

You seek God, everything else automatically follows. Then why do we need to seek other things anyway? But how can we seek him when we are filled with pride, which makes us think we do not need God? We are trying to find answers to mysterious things using our logic, knowledge, and understanding to the point of questioning God's existence. But if we humble ourselves and seek God—and Jesus—we will know that there is power in the name of Jesus who won all the life's battles for us. And then, if we trust in His name we will be victorious in everything we do. Our lives are completely transformed and then we will also be willing to do anything that Jesus tells us to do.

God never forgets His promises,
His people—it is us who forget.

# Pride Can Invade with or without Our Consent

Every day when I think of writing this book, I feel I really do not have anything anymore to write, but then suddenly I start getting thoughts that I do not even think about. Today again, when I got up in the morning, I started my day as usual, meditating, and these thoughts came which I am writing.

I was thinking our prayers get answered when we pray, even though I feel many times they need not be answered. We certainly do not deserve that our prayers should be answered; then I question why our prayers are answered even when we are so unfaithful and disobedient. God tells us to do something we do not do, in fact we use our own logic and do exactly opposite to what God has said, yet he answers our prayers. Why? It actually shows the goodness and the characteristics of God that he is so loving, forgiving, and compassionate that even I do not have the words to describe. Then what is our conclusion? We feel we are so right-eous before God that he has answered our prayers, and most often invite spiritual pride to step in us. We forget and ignore the fact that it is all because of his grace, mercy, and love that those prayers are answered. And we, even the so-called believers, become proud of ourselves knowing that the one who created the universe has listened to us.

As a teenager, once I had asked God to show me that he really existed by making me get honor roll in my tenth grade, which he did, and which was very important to me at that time. That was my first step to build a relationship with him. I was then very innocent but at the same time very adamant that if God really existed then he should manifest to me. Now when I look back, I ask myself how I could dare to ask that question to God. I feel I was silly, stupid, but at that time I think even God did not think that it was a stupid question, because that night he had done more than what I had asked or expected him to do. He had not only showed me my actual marks card with honor roll numbers but also had shown himself and made me hear him speak, which at that time I never shared with anyone, as I myself was not sure of what I had experienced.

So when I first got that prayer answered, I was filled with a lot of pride. I thought, *Even God, the creator of this universe, had listened to me. I must be really great.* I took everything in the wrong way. There was nobody who could lead me in the right direction as I had not shared my experience with God with anyone, not even the closest people in my life.

At that time I was of the belief that faith and God is a very private, personal thing. We do not have to show or tell anyone or everyone what, who, and how much we believe. I knew I believe in God and that was enough for me, but in the Bible, Mark 8:38 says, "Whosoever therefore shall be ashamed of me and of my words in this adulterous and sinful generation; of him also shall the Son of man be ashamed when he cometh in the glory of his Father." It clearly says we have to confess our faith in front of people openly without any shame or regret. God wants us to glorify his name by declaring his works in our lives. He says, "and my glory will I not give to another" (Isaiah 42:8).

Many times in the Bible it is written, especially in the book of Psalms, "Declare my works among the people, make known my name among the nations." Since I was not aware of the Scriptures at that time in detail, I did not do all that. I was not really ashamed of him—Jesus—but was ignorant; as such I was content and happy with what I knew about God and what he had done for me. I started feeling proud of myself as God had fulfilled every desire of my heart that I presented before him. So then because of those answered prayers, I had slowly started judging people, their faith, and sometimes even condemning them. The worst part was that I did not feel anything wrong doing that. I used to think something happened to people, or people's prayers did not get answered because of their lack of faith or something that they did wrong, and so on. I myself hardly knew about God, still I was the one trying to judge and justify.

God had only showed me that indeed he existed by doing what I had required of him, yet I took pride in that innocently, of course, in the beginning, but as I started believing in him more and more and every time that I prayed, more of my prayers got answered. Pride stepped in my life and slowly built itself a strong home in my heart. I did not think that my prayers were answered because of my innocent prayer and faith, because of my humbleness and sincerity. I took that in a wrong way—felt myself being great. God gave me many opportunities to get rid of my pride, but would I listen? No way. He tried to teach me without having to hurt me, but I was nowhere close to listening to him. He then gave me up to my stubborn heart. Maybe God must have thought that someday I will change my mind then obey and humble myself. He does not like to impose himself on us; that freedom to choose he has given to foolish people like us who cannot even differentiate between evil and good on our own. We are blindfolded by the external forces of this world so much that we cannot even see the results of the choices that we make in our lives.

See, God tells us once, twice, and then he lets us have what we desire. But if he thinks of us as his children, he certainly knows how to bring us back to him. In my case, when he saw that I am going way far from him, he finally decided to do something, which I am sure he must have wished he did not have to do. God never forgets his promises, his people, it is us who forget.

I had forgotten the "dangerous prayer" that I had prayed when I took my first step toward God as a teenager, but which he had remembered. I had then said to him, "Lord, if I ever go away from you, then do something in my life that will make me come back to you. Do not ever make me so comfortable in life that will make me forget about you in my life." As such, God taught me a lesson that I would never forget. He made me feel the pain that I had made him feel by using the most precious thing in my life—my firstborn son—by making him disobey. The child that I loved so much became rebellious and disobeyed me so much to the point that I could not solve the situation on my own, not even with anybody's help.

I never listened to people when they told me that I was proud. I never agreed—just said people do not know me, that is why they are saying that, until finally God made me realize that I indeed was proud. He used the most precious thing in my life to bring me back on the right track. My only son, the one I was so proud of, the one I loved so much, the one I played with, the one I even shared my joys, my sorrows when he was just a baby, though he could not understand anything at the time. He always was a great brother for my daughter, Nikeeta, and a great son to us, so I had a special bond with him. But when he did what I never expected of him in my life, it dawned on me what I did to God, not realizing how much I hurt him. I had promised to God that I will be faithful to him if he shows me that he exists, which he did by doing what I had asked him to do, yet I had not kept that promise which I had made on my own free will.

I was the most precious thing for God when I had said to him, "I will believe in you if you show me that you exist," and had submitted myself to him as his child to take care of me when I had seen with my own eyes what he had done, yet I did not keep my promise. I was complaining of my son when he had just disobeyed me, of which he had not even promised, and here I was disobeying the Almighty God to whom I had promised that I will always abide in him and depend on him, yet had not realized rather accepted that anything was even wrong. There was no way God could give up on me. He is a God who is willing to work on you to keep you from perishing even if you show a little sign that you are willing to turn toward him. So, he had to do something. He had said, "I will not never leave thee nor forsake thee" (Hebrews 13:5). As such, he made me suffer not to destroy me but to bring me back on the right track, to bless me more, because even through that trial with my son he promised me when he spoke loudly about my son, Vincent, "I have chosen him. Do not worry," But by this time, God had made me admit that I was indeed proud, and when I asked forgiveness, he easily forgave.

I had done the initial step of obedience by taking water baptism, which I was refusing for more than twenty-plus years because of one simple reason—I was under the impression that I was already baptized as a child, as is done in many denominations, until God revealed to me that I was not. Baptism is something we willingly make a choice to take when we understand fully the meaning of that word, thus showing in action our understanding of that word. It was only after I obeyed that commandment of God that my life had changed completely. See, taking water baptism itself is not significant because it is just dipping in water, but the obedience and humbleness that comes with that is what makes the difference. Of course it could become a ritual also if it is done for the sake of tradition, but if we do that after understanding the significance of that word, then only our lives are changed. It actually requires humbleness to do that. So, for me, it was only after that step of obedience of water baptism that initiated conversations with God. It was not one-way conversations anymore. I started to hear from God and talk to him back, which at first I thought was my imagination. I thought maybe I am attending too many prayer meetings or getting too spiritual or was crazy. I was talking to him as I would talk to any other person—sometimes in audible voice—felt myself drunk of which I wanted more and more.

It was a wonderful experience which made me so happy. I could rejoice; my tears of sorrow had turned to tears of joy even though my situation had not changed, my son was still the same. I could not understand anything; all I knew was my burden was lifted off my shoulder. At that time I had received another promise, i.e, "All my children will be taught by God." What more could I ask or want? I knew then I just have to trust in his promise and wait for him to make everything beautiful in his time.

During this period, God had started asking me to do certain things, which was again difficult for me to do even though everyone of them I did reluctantly, as it had become my desire to be obedient, especially after knowing what disobedience had cost me. It took three years to see the change in my son's life to testify. It did not happen because I had put the time frame but maybe because God must have decided my son does not have to suffer because of me. It also helped my son to become who he is today; he is much more closer to God than I ever was at that age and he is now known by people as "Fire for God."

On our recent visit to India, a prayer meeting was arranged in one of the local churches where my son was invited to speak which was kind of unexpected but he had shared his testimony and God's word which was truly a blessing to many people. After the meeting, we were invited to visit one of my extended family— where just a casual talk led to conversation on baptism. That family had asked a question to my son, "Is it necessary to get baptized?" Many people argue on this subject extensively and explain by giving many examples but my son just said very simply and quoted scriptures.

Jesus said, "_ If ye love me, keep my command-ments." (John 14:15). As for baptism, no matter how much and however we argue, that is one of the things Jesus said to do (Mark 16:15–16). And so if we claim we truly love Jesus, we need to do as he says; otherwise we can be very well labeled as hypocrites. There is nothing to argue—it is up to people whether they choose to do or not to do. Actually I was kind of getting excited to witness some big explanation and argument on that sub-ject but to my disappointment that's all my son said and that was the end of that conversation. I was just dumbfounded hearing such a meaningful but simple explanation of baptism especially since I was expecting a big commotion. A couple of weeks later, we came to know that person went and took water baptism. Very interesting and amazing are God's works, all glory and praises go to him. He works in mysterious ways and he has an appointed time for everything.

God has blessed me and my family so much in ways that I could not even imagine especially after I humbled myself before him. He has blessed both my children with so many talents; now it is my prayer that he makes use of those talents for his glory. It is my earnest prayer that pride will never make a way in their lives which had caused me so much pain, which had made me lose all my blessings without my knowledge or consent. I do not want my children or anybody going through the experience that I went through. Can you imagine God can even forgive sins like adultery if we ask forgiveness? But pride, I think it's very difficult for him to forgive. It is because adultery we commit one time; we learn lesson from it. Chances are we probably will never do that again. But pride, it comes and gets us even if and when we decide we do not want to be part of it.

Pride is something that comes very easily. We achieve something, we become proud. We get good job, we become proud. Our kids do something extraordinary or nice, we become proud. Our God does something for us, we become proud, and so on. It is a never-ending list. It is so easy for Satan to make a way into our lives through pride. Satan knows God hates pride, because of which he makes us to fall as a prey to that easily and repeatedly. If we read the Bible we see that everyone, no matter how blessed anybody was, whoever had pride, God destroyed that person. There are several examples in the Bible that shows pride causes destruction. It did not really matter what position someone had or what good or bad that person did. God did not even spare Lucifer, the fallen angel, when he became proud. As such, God had to destroy him. He is then referred to as Satan, who first tempted

Eve to sin, and still continues to do so.

We all know we should not have pride, yet we do. So what can we do to prevent pride ruling our lives? The only way to save ourselves from pride is to follow Jesus, who is the perfect example of humbleness, and to abide in him at all times. The minute we get away from him, we open the wide door for Satan to make his way through pride in our lives. What can be more easier for him?

Take the example of a child, who is so innocent and humble, but as he grows up he gets knowledge, understanding, which makes him feel he can do everything by himself, or he feels he is better than others. Then slowly pride steps in his life with or without his consent. And then as we harbor pride in us without acknowledging, it causes us to sin; in fact it can give birth to all sins. Children do not have pride but adults do, especially those who grow up leading their lives without God. Pride is the beginning of sin, which is not easy to be convicted or convinced of. It is very subtle, invisible many times. So once you let pride that God hates rule your life, then nobody can convince you of that—leading to all the deadly sins—except God himself, who is the only one who can save you from destroying your life.

# What Do We Need in the End?

One day I came from work. My husband was watching a movie called *Moses*. I started watching with him for some time. As I was watching, it made me think—God provided Moses every luxury that he could have, even though he was born to poor parents. He let him enjoy everything in a worldly way, made him so strong physically, mentally, in every aspect that he started to believe in his strength—himself. Pride invaded him. That is when God took him to places he had never been before, made him suffer so much that he lost all his human strength. But God protected and provided for him, only after which he humbled himself to a certain point—it took forty years. It was then God appeared to him, telling him of his purpose for him, thereafter Moses received strength that he never had before. Moses then accepted how lowly he was in front of God when he encountered Him at a personal level, when everything was revealed to him. Yet because God chose him, he was just dumbfounded. After that, he knew what he did was not from his own strength but someone greater than him and everybody else. This kind of experience comes only with a personal encounter with God. No other person can explain to anybody nor make anyone understand.

Moses is the only one that is mentioned in Bible who I would say received the longest training from God for eighty years before he started to do what God had called him for. He lived to be 120 years, out of which forty years he lived in pure luxury, then forty years in suffering, and then the next forty years in the wilderness doing God's work, which I think must have been the most satisfying years of his life. Yet he was not able to see the promised land—again it is still not clear why. Was it because of pride leading to disobedience, distrust, refusal to accept his mistake, blaming other people instead, or something else? (Numbers 20:1–13 and Deuteronomy 4:21) Of course, it was because of sin but what led him to sin.

My personal opinion, at least in the beginning, was that he was not only proud but also a very short-tempered man. God trained him to be humble but then when I questioned God why he did not reach the promised land, the answer came back as *pride* even though scripture says it was distrust. But God himself testifies of Moses as being the humble servant (Numbers 12:3). What is written in the Scriptures cannot be conflicting, but that does raise a question—the answer of which can only be given by God himself! Maybe when the Scriptures were translated from one language to another or from one version to another the meaning of some words got farther away from the original literal Hebrew translation, that's why when we read the Scriptures, it is better to ask the Holy Spirit to reveal the message.

I was just thinking, *Why do we even take pride in anything anyway?* If we look around us, then we will find that there is always someone who is better than us, someone smarter and more intelligent than us, someone who is more beautiful than us, someone who is more talented than us, someone who is more prosperous than us, etc. If we do not find someone like that, then know that the world we are living in is too small. We need to expand our horizons, then only we will be able to see ourselves—how lowly we are and where we stand. Humbleness will automatically follow.

Nothing in this world belongs to us; even the next breath to be alive we cannot control. Everything that we have is because of the grace of our Almighty God. We came from dust and we will go back to dust. We came with nothing to this earth when we were born, and we will not take anything when we go from this earth when we die. We do not even know if we will be alive the next second. As it says in James 4:14, "Whereas ye know not what shall be on the morrow. For what is your life?" Even then, we plan for the future, try to make and save money, build big mansions, accumulate things, property that we do not even know if we'll ever use them or whether we will be there to enjoy them. But what we may need in the end is maybe a 2 × 6 feet land to be buried, or a little bigger, as is said in one of the Hindi movies, *Prem Nagar*. Out of that three-hour movie that I had watched long back, all I had remembered was that sentence that had made me think of so many things. Even that is not necessary if we think about it as we will not even feel anything after our death anyway. Then I thought, What are we working for? Who are we working for? Why are we losing our peace and joy in doing something that we may not even enjoy? We hear about people, even family members, fighting over a piece of land or money to the point of even killing them. All that to get what? Would we be able to enjoy our life then? Won't we feel guilty for the rest of our lives?

All is vanity. Even then, we have the nerve to take pride and say we have so much such and such things. I have known many people who have big houses, who have everything that money can buy in those houses, but are they enjoying? Of course not, because there is nobody in the house to enjoy. But instead people who visit them enjoy as the owners do not have time because they are too busy working to make money to pay the huge bills for the maintenance of those houses. Or else they have so much wealth that they feel insecure that it takes away their sleep, the peace that they could otherwise have. It makes me remember a sentence from another movie, "-*Deewar*"- that I watched years back, it was said we cannot make money if we get good sleep and if we do make money then we do not get good sleep. How true is it? Isn't that something we should all ponder about? I am not against getting wealthy or living a comfortable life, but I just want you to think of getting your priorities straight in your life. Do not run after things of this world that will make your lives miserable, but instead opt for heavenly blessings.

We strive so hard to get more and more. In the beginning maybe it is a necessity. Slowly it develops into our character, giving us the desire to have more and more. Then when we get everything that we could get—what money can buy—and we feel we cannot get anything more, then we begin to feel inadequate, depressed, because now we cannot get rid of that character that had developed over the years to get more and more things that money can buy. That is how we hear of many wealthy, famous people, in spite of having everything, are lonely and unhappy. Then the next thing we hear, they committed suicide or got into drugs or alcohol, and ended up dying one fine day.

People can never get satisfied living the worldly way. The only way we can get satisfied is when we seek the Lord, when we remember the God who created us, who can satisfy us with everlasting food both physically and spiritually, and we start depending on him for every need of ours. Then we will experience the joy and peace that nothing in this world can be compared to; and depending on how much we are right with God or how God chooses to bless us, we will have the material blessings in the worldly terms also. But whatever God decides to give, it is a sure thing that we will be content with what he gives, how much he gives, and we will enjoy life with little or more, whatever we will have. And then if we surrender ourselves to the one who gave it all and acknowledge that grace, then I think we would be the most blessed persons on the earth. People will envy us for that. Is that life easy to live? Of course not. We want to get something? Then we will have to give something. We have to surrender our *will* to God to live a successful life like that, which is a very difficult thing to do.

One of life's most important things is *will* which defines us, gives us a unique personality, but that's the thing God is asking us to give up. We are basically giving up the right to live in a literal sense if we give up our will to somebody's will, but that is what God wants us to do. He expects us to make the decision on our free will to give ourselves to him and let him take complete charge of our lives. That is what I have done, and I'll assure you that if you make that decision then that will be the best decision you can make, which I can guarantee you will never regret for the rest of your life.

It says in the Bible that God created us in his image, and so every time when I think of giving an example, I cannot think anything better than human relationships. See, it is like a parent-child relationship; every parent has desire to teach their children the right things and love their children equally. But think of how our children grow and live. When they are little, they love to do everything we ask them to do, even though we don't realize that they are rebellious the moment they are born. That little baby is capable of manipulating us as parents according to his or her needs and we feel happy to be manipulated so as to satisfy that baby's needs, not knowing when that baby grows up how he or she might turn out. Anyway, as our children grow we enjoy every moment; even if they are not doing everything our way, we still are okay with that because they are still doing what we want them to do. Then still as they grow they desire to be more independent, and many times they do things that we do not want them to do. Then we do not enjoy as much but still we wish the best for them. Our heart yearns that they should turn back from their wrong ways and do the right things. Some children may turn out to be obedient while others may not, depending on various reasons and their personalities, as everyone is created unique. So then slowly when they fail to do the right things, then sin steps in them; and as they grow like that in their adulthood, they become responsible for their acts and are held accountable for the consequences of their sins. Then they cannot do anything but pay the price, whatever it is, with whatever they have.

It is the same thing with God. He has given us the *word of God* as our instruction book, and he expects us to obey his commandments. But when we don't then obviously we are held accountable for our acts. Do parents enjoy their children going astray like that? Definitely not. Then how can God enjoy his children going astray? But the children have made that choice by not listening what they had heard or by being disobedient. It says in the Bible, "Train up a child in the way he should go:

and when he is old, he will not depart from it."
(Proverbs 22:6). Everything that the Scriptures
says, it is true—it works. I can say that because I
have experienced many things in my life.

I thought I had brought up my children in a
good Christian way which my son even acknowledges ; I had taught them to read the Bible, pray,
go to church, attend Sunday school. Even then
*when my son became a teenager, he* became disobedient, because of which our family had to suffer a
lot. Maybe partly it was my fault as I had opened
a wide door for pride to step in my heart, which is
perhaps the worst sin that I realize now, and also
partly because God had chosen my son for his purpose, and I think he wanted to mold him in the
way he wanted. Even though my son went astray
hanging out with the wrong group of people, but
he never forgot the teachings that I had taught
him as a child. One time when I was feeling so
depressed, crying, I was asking myself, *Where had
I gone wrong? What did I do so bad that I am in a
situation like this?* Even at this point I could not
bring myself to say it was my pride. Then my son
told me, "Mama, don't worry about me. You have
brought me up to be a good Christian man—I will
be okay." I wanted to believe that but could not. I
was so upset that day that I decided to drop my son
home and just go somewhere. But my son that day

was not willing to leave me alone thinking that I might do something to hurt myself until I promised him that I will not. At times like that, I was often reminded of the promise about my son that I had heard from God—"I have chosen him. Do not worry"—but the fact that my son was not doing what I was expecting him to do was not acceptable to me or the society, so it was hard for me to believe what I had heard. But three years after, I had to believe what God had said is what I had heard because my son has come so close to God in ways that I would never have thought or dreamed.

My son always was and is a very loving person going out of his way to help others even if it meant to go out of his comfort zone. He had a good, generous, sincere heart, and I think that is what God looks in people when he decides to use them for his works, for his glory, but he has his own way of molding and using them.. Even though many times I tell my son to grow up but in my heart I always wish he does not give up the heart of a child which allows him to meet God. Today I feel so blessed and relieved to know that my son has chosen God above everything else and he has the passion for him in ways that even I never had especially at that age. As I said earlier, when I was praying for my son, I was given another promise that my children will be taught by God, which included my daughter. I was so happy my burden was lifted off; what more did I need! Can anyone be more blessed than the one who is taught by God himself, the creator of this universe, who knows ins and outs of every human being and everything? I thought now I do not have to discipline my children as that responsibility of mine God has taken. I now claim that promise every day in my prayers for them. He deals with everybody on individual bases. My daughter is also blessed with many talents, and I am sure God will use her also for his glory. I know she has faith and so much boldness that she could stand up for that cause against her own mother, which she has proved once at a very young age. I pray that she also has passion for God beyond everything else. Then I will also be able to say, "And as for me and my household, we will serve the Lord," as Joshua had said in the Old Testament (Joshua 24:15).

Me and my household will serve the Lord in the coming days, as it is my earnest prayer—my house will be called as "house of prayer" someday—when people will see the prayers answered and acknowledge Jesus as their God and savior through our lives.

It says in Proverbs 23:26,
"My son, give me thine heart, and let
thine eyes observe my ways."

# Choosing to Surrender to the Wrong Master!

I had everything in my life—a loving home; beautiful, talented, intelligent children, good jobs; a husband who loved me so much—what more could I desire or need in my life? The day I forgot that all these things are because of God, on whom I was so much dependent but that I had begun to take for granted—the day *pride* came in my heart and life—that was the end of my blessings.

I did not even realize when pride had made its way through in me. Like I said, Satan is very subtle and sneaky. He will make you feel nothing is wrong by doing something wrong the first time then he will make you repeat those mistakes, which otherwise you wouldn't do them. I did not even stop to think that pride was something God hates, which is said many times throughout the Bible. Satan had mesmerized me so much that it made me forget my favorite verse—"Pride goeth before destruction" (Proverbs 16:18). I did not acknowledge of my pride in everything that I did until God took a step in my life and made me realize that he never liked pride, but it took a long time—twenty-plus years. God had brought many situations in my life to which if I had paid any attention I would have known that he was trying to discipline me, but I could not get that message. It was because Satan had a strong hold on me. As soon as he saw that I will be vulnerable through pride he left no chance of making me fall into a trap that he had carefully prepared for me to drift away from God. God had made me go through the difficult situations in my family life, which made me realize that what I was doing was not right in his sight, but still he did not take away the freedom to choose from me. I still was free to choose and am very glad that finally I had made the right choice, i.e, to get rid of my pride, which was a barrier between me and him, which enabled me to humble myself enough to come before God, thus ask for forgiveness.

I once again surrendered my life to him, this time with an understanding of my devotion to him with all my heart, mind, and soul. I took water baptism, which was my first step of showing obedience to God, as I was rebelling against that for the long twenty-plus years. I swore that Satan will never again take me away from God—not this time—because now I am a new person in Christ. The battle is not between me and Satan anymore; it is between God and Satan. God had defeated him before, and he will defeat him every time, so now he is the one who will be fighting the battles for me.

I am here to do God's will and purpose no matter what happens now. I was dead but now am alive; I caught a glimpse of heaven when God took me to heaven with him in a vision. It was a beautiful place. But still I felt uncomfortable as when I looked around, saw many people walking to and fro in front of me; they looked very happy but could not find anyone that I knew personally. Then I found myself seated next to Jesus. Can you imagine that? I had been given so much importance in heaven. But that is when he showed the people who were lost, after which he told me to go down and do his work on earth. I did not want to do that thinking my seat next to Jesus will be lost, but when he showed me how many people on earth were still living in the dark, especially the people I knew, I could not bring myself to say no. Suddenly I had the passion for the lost ones and readily agreed to do what God wanted me to do. Finally he made me understand his purpose and will for me, for my life that he created. Now the joy that I get knowing that one more soul has been freed from the clutches of Satan through me or through somebody else and has entered the kingdom of God is unexplainable. Now I understand the importance of making the divine choices; thus, I have the desire to choose the right master. But there are still people here who are making the wrong choices that I had made in my life. This is because of the power of pride that they still have in their lives, because of which I am writing this book.

Perhaps God will talk to someone who reads this book of my journey of life with pride, passing through a phase of destruction and ultimately leading to blessings because of my repentance and his grace. But the grace period will not last forever because the second coming of Jesus is very near. This time, he will come not as a helpless baby but as a judge when he will not give time for repentance, so the time is now to make that important decision of your lives.

I am glad that I had made that decision. I decided this time Satan will not win with me because now he will have to pass through my God to reach me. He got me once and I paid the price for that by Jesus's blood through whom God had redeemed me of that sin. It will not happen again, as now I understand and feel the pain that Jesus had to endure for my disobedience. He still needs to refine me, make me pure and holy enough, cleanse me completely with his precious blood that he shed on that cross for my sins so that I can abide in him and he can dwell in me. It says in Proverbs 23:26, "My son, give me thine heart, and let thine eyes observe my ways." You know why God wants our heart? It is because the heart is wicked; it can devise evil things that we may not even be aware of. The only way we can have a pure heart is when we have a good relationship with God. To have that, we need to have a clean heart. If our heart is right with God, then only we can hear him speak, and he will hear us speak to him. Then we will start experiencing the blessings, miracles giving us the happiness and peace that no one can ever give.

I am writing this book so that nobody has to go through what I went through because of pride. Believe me, it is very unpleasant but if that is the only way you will listen and come closer to God, by experiencing the pain, then pray that you will, because it is still worth all the pain, anguish, humiliation. God will exalt you eventually.

We had a very young preacher in one of our other local churches—his name was Ashish. I remember something he had said in one of his sermons. That is some people are obedient on their own, some are made obedient by others, and some are made obedient by God. The ones who are disciplined by God are most likely to be the most obedient people as they will never forget the spanking that God gives, which, of course, will be very unpleasant. He gives many opportunities before he even thinks of disciplining us, to make us turn away from the wrong things of the world through many ways. Because he knows when he sees us suffer he suffers even more which he certainly does not want to do but some people like me are so stubborn that it does not go into thick head and brain of ours that God has no choice but to spank us. We push him so much that he has to do what he does not want to do. By disobeying, we not only suffer but people around us suffer too. We make him suffer also as he is the most loving God, full of love, mercy, and kindness. Not because we deserve all those things, but because he loves us so much that he does not want even one of us to perish, and he wants every soul to come back to him but on one's free will and choice.

You may recall the parable that Jesus shared with people about the lost sheep (Luke 15:3–7). He tells that a certain man had one hundred sheep but when one of them got lost, he left all those ninety-nine sheep and went to look for the one sheep that was lost. He could have easily said, *What is just one sheep? I still have 99 sheep. Why bother looking for the lost disobedient sheep?* but he did not do that. Instead he left all those other sheep to look for that one lost sheep. He did not rest until he found it, and then the story says he rejoiced. In other words, God does not want even a single soul to get lost. He loves us so much that it will hurt him deeply if he is unable to gather all the lost ones. We are living in his grace period, but there will come a time when that grace will not be available. That is why he wants to gather all his sheep; in other words, the lost ones who are still living in the dark, before the grace period is over by sending people to them, giving them messages through different ways. Sadly even then people are not willing to listen, but those who do will be saved and considered wise in the sight of God. Let us not take his grace and love for granted.

One Thanksgiving Day, after prayer and food, as a church we were watching a movie—I forgot the name—but it was all about making choices in life. Every choice we make there is a consequence for that—it can be good or bad depending on our decision to choose. It made me reflect on my life— the choices I had made. Many times I knew what I was doing was wrong; even then I was trying to justify them by using my logic, my understanding and my knowledge. Everything was about me, of me, and by me. If we see the word pride, it is all about "I" or "me" in the middle? (that's how Sister Manisha worded it also when I had asked her to speak something on pride) and when that happens nobody can convince you that you are wrong—you can be wrong, you could be wrong, you may be wrong. Even if you agree with people, still you will not be willing to listen and accept—that is the power of *pride*.

It took a long time for me to make the right choice. I could not do it until God himself intervened in my life. I could not admit that I had pride until he made me realize that. Once I realized, everything else was easy to do. I could repent, humble myself before God and people, which led me toward obedience that God was waiting for me to do. And then there was no turning back, my burden was lifted off, my problems were taken care of. He started to guide and counsel me in every little thing that I did. Every decision made by me was then based on his counsel. The joy and the peace that God gave me was beyond my understanding—no words will be able to explain that feeling. It is something everyone should experience. I would not trade that for any luxury or anything of this world. It is a divine gift from God to his obedient children.

The best thing is that anyone in this world can receive that gift provided we do what we are expected. It is very simple yet very difficult to do, especially if we have pride in our hearts, i.e., to choose to serve the right master. For which we first have to learn to know about him and develop a relationship with him by having faith in him, which comes by hearing the word of God. Romans 10:17 says, "So then faith cometh by hearing, and hearing by the word of God." That means we need to spend time in God's presence every day just as we do with any of our loved ones, which helps us build healthy and strong relationships. We cannot expect a relationship to flourish if we do not give our time and energy for it.

Speaking in tongues is one of the signs of being baptized in the Holy Spirit. It is one of the gifts. It is not something that one should boast about but instead, be thankful to God for that gift.

# Does God Talk Only If We Speak in Tongues?

People used to make me feel very uncomfortable when they prayed in tongues especially when they made me feel that I could not talk to God if I didn't speak in tongues. Many considered themselves being better than me because of that reason, and they would show that in action, which made me resent the so-called believers. I tried to stay away from such believers, used to think of them as hypocrites because they portrayed of being proud of themselves even though they claimed otherwise.

I always thought whosoever is in Christ cannot and should not have pride in them because Christ himself lived as the most humble person, which he showed by his works and behavior. So I labeled these so-called believers, who claimed to talk to God, as hypocrites because of their pride. Whenever I entered their group of "believers," the first thing that they would ask is, "Are you saved or do you speak in tongues or did you get baptized by the Holy Spirit?" and if my answer was no, then their behavior toward me would be quite different. Then they would make me feel as if I was the biggest sinner that lived on the face of this earth. On the other hand, if my answer was yes, then they would treat me so nicely as if I belonged to their own family. I felt that was not right—that's not how Jesus treated people. In fact Jesus says that he came for the sinners. Now don't get me wrong as I am sure not all believers are like that.

Anyway, ever since I experienced God in my life, my attitude toward these people changed, especially when he started to reveal things to me, started talking to me. God created everyone to be different—we cannot expect the same behavior from different people in any group. I was reminded of the parable of the ten lepers that Jesus heals but then only one leper comes back to Jesus to give thanks (Luke 17:11–19). You can read the full story in that chapter. I was wondering and questioning why all those ten lepers didn't come back to give thanks to Jesus. They all got healed the same way at the same time, right? It made me realize then that there may be many believers who believe in God but only one that actually follows the teachings of the Lord, follows in his footsteps. One of the fruits of the Spirit is humbleness. When there is humbleness there is no room for pride. Speaking in tongues is one of the signs of being baptized in the Holy Spirit. It is one of the gifts. There is nothing that one should be proud of but instead be thankful to God for that. That gift is given not to boast about or to put someone down but rather to edify themselves to produce the fruits of the spirit and even intercede through that gift for other people.

I wrote little bit of my thoughts about Scriptures in *Jesusnatyam* my first book, i.e., the Scriptures or Bible is written by the inspiration of the Holy Spirit revealed to certain chosen people, thus conveyed the message of God. Does that mean God has stopped talking and choosing people to convey his messages? Absolutely not, because he is still doing that, but the Scriptures, or the Bible itself, is complete in itself. It talks about the beginning and the end; it clearly states nothing should be added or removed, whosoever does that will be punished (Revelation 23). But God has not stopped speaking or revealing things to people. He still does that but those need not be recorded in the Scriptures; everything that is revealed to us is already there in Scriptures, but many times the secrets are revealed through those words. I often question myself— Did Jesus speak in tongues? It is not mentioned in the Bible—maybe he did or didn't, but I know for sure, as is written, he certainly talked to God the Father.

God still talks. I have experienced this, so have many people. I have heard the audible voice. I do not speak in tongues, so I cannot say how the Holy Spirit, whom many have experienced, sounds or feels like. It is not that I do not believe people who have been baptized by the Holy spirit do show the physical evidence of speaking in tongues—maybe they do—maybe that is how they communicate with God and edify themselves...but is that the only evidence? And then, to talk to God, is it necessary to speak in tongues? We do not have to, that I know for sure. Because most of the time when talking to or hearing from God, I hear in English, complete sentences. Many times he asks me to do things, which is in plain English. God speaks the language that you and I can understand. He would never leave us puzzled. It took quite a long time for me to recognize that voice. I had struggled hard trying to discern the voice of God until he made me hear, "It is me." It was then that I could actually say that what I was hearing was from God. I would not put myself as Doubting Thomas, but at the same time I wanted to be 100 percent sure that "it was God."

Since all this experience was new for me I used to ask people for their advice. People who seemed to know God had confused me so much about what we could hear with all the different voices that were out there. But I do not think I had heard any voice other than God's, the reason being first of all, when I heard him speak the first time, I did not even know there were other voices to hear. Then it was my earnest prayer to God (once I knew there were other voices to hear) that if I hear anything it should be only his voice. I had no desire to hear anything else at all.

Many times I even prayed to God like this, "Lord, I do not want to hear anything especially about things that do not concern me just tell me about me and my family." But even then he revealed to me about other things, other people that did not concern me, many times about people in other cities even other countries. Then I realized God is even more eager to talk to us than we to him. See, he looks for people who have the desire to talk and listen to him. I had a desire so deep to experience talking to him—how much desire even I did not know myself, but I just wanted to hear about myself, my children, my family, nothing else, but God does not work that way. He does not say, "Okay, I talked about what you wanted to talk and hear, and so now I will stop talking." No, he still wants to talk, wants to share everything he has, the burden he has, his joy, his sorrow, especially when he sees people's wicked ways, for he knows the out-come of their acts. He wants to tell people through people who are willing to convey his message that they should turn toward him and trust him. And that is how we get burden for sharing the gospel and have the desire to bring at least one more soul to his kingdom.

I have not seen anyone who is truly saved who does not have the desire to save others. Can man save somebody? Of course not; but man can make a way for God to do the work for him. Our job is to show the *way*—that is *Jesus* (John 14:6). Whether people choose the *way* or not, it is their choice. If God did not force people to make a choice, then who are we to do so? But we can tell people about the good news—the way to salvation—and leave the rest up to that person.

Okay, coming back to baptism; the Scriptures clearly states that the Holy Spirit wants us to get baptized. We receive the Holy Spirit the time we accept Jesus, but we need the anointing of the Holy Spirit to attain the power of the Holy Spirit to do God's will and work. Otherwise, we will be fearful or do not have the boldness needed. Again, is speaking in holy tongues the only evidence of getting baptized in the Holy Spirit? That I do not know for sure; yet what I do know is that when we get baptized in the Holy Spirit, we receive the power to do God's will, which may be beyond our abilities, and he will guide us through every step and make a way for what he has called us for. He will equip us with everything that we need to overcome all our weaknesses to do his work. It could be the unusual talent that we never thought we had, or exercising our inborn talent that we already have, only now using them to glorify God, which is the right purpose.

Have I received the anointing of the Holy Spirit? Every time I ask God, in answer to my question he directs me to the verse where it says, "The Spirit of the Lord God is upon me; because the Lord has hath anointed me," (Isaiah 61:1) which leads me to believe that maybe I am anointed. Because I do now have the boldness to tell people or write whatever he asks me to write, I am writing these books that I never dreamed I will be writing in my life. I am willing to sing for him when I never sang in my life before and have many times shared thoughts in my church as the Spirit had led me even though it was against my nature, though reluctantly in the beginning, but did eventually. Still I can't say 100 percent if I have received the anointing rather overflow of the anointing, because if I did then I should be able to do even more works as per God's commandment in spreading the gospel in whatever way I can, maybe then I could say, "Yes, I have received the anointing."

Some people say crying is also a gift. Again I cry all the time, which I never used to do before. People used to say my heart is made of stone. Now I cry so easily—cry when I hear the messages that touch my heart, when I hear the songs that touch me, when I feel the sufferings of Jesus for my sins, when I see my prayers are answered without uttering a word. I cannot pray without crying because when I pray I just go out of control, have tears that I pray with, no words come out. A lot of times people ask me the reason for my crying, for which I don't have any explanation. In moments like that, I feel God's presence so much that it makes me want that time to stand still and at that moment I am willing to trade anything of this world for him. It is a beautiful experience, so precious, and I pray that everyone in this world should experience that.

God has taught me to be humble enough to hear his voice. It didn't happen overnight but many days of shedding tears of repentance for having pride in me that God hates. Finally, one fine day he said very clearly, "Your sins are forgiven," and it is written in the Bible in Psalm 32:1, "Blessed is he whose transgressions are is forgiven." And then I heard, "From heaven I made you hear my voice" (Deuteronomy 4:36).

Some of the Scripture readings that I have quoted in this book or my previous book are the ones that I have heard through God speaking to me directly because until then I was unaware of those verses as I had not read the Bible. I started reading them only after I had heard those verses as I was getting inquisitive to find those verses in the Scriptures which made me read one of the most fascinating books of all times, the Bible. I still have not read the whole Bible as many might have done. Actually I was told by some people that we should read the Bible from the beginning to the end atleast once in our lifetime. Believe me I even tried my best to do that but I was unable to do so. It was because many times I cannot even read the whole chapter let alone read the sixty-six books. I am made to stop reading at one verse then that's it...I cannot go further but whatever I read makes room in my heart which stays for good. Ofcourse I did read most of the books of the Bible but now it does not matter anymore because anything that I read, God talks to me through that.

It says, "But seek ye first the kingdom of God, and his righteousness; and all these things shall be added unto you." (Matthew 6:33). So, if we choose God and everything else will automatically follow, then think about it—Why should we choose something else anyway? I am not at all implying that we should be choosing him because of that as prime reason. We should choose him because he is worthy to be chosen for what he has done for us, or just for the reason that he chose us first. Who does not want a God who is so awesome, loving, compassionate and forgiving, who is everything that a person wants or needs, after which there are no wants or needs left?

# Godly Love versus Worldly Love

People in this world are selfish, no matter how much we claim to love another person. When we are driven to a certain point, we still have the tendency to stop loving that person. What I am trying to say is that there are limitations, expectations with man that no matter how much a person claims that he loves somebody, when they cross a certain limit, their love diminishes and eventually fades away. There is a big difference between godly love and worldly love; actually pride comes in between. Worldly love wants to take something from others but godly love wants to give something to others. Only people who are humble are able to show God's love. True love does not know pride. In Scriptures, 1 Corinthians 13:4–5 explains that one of the characteristics of God's love is humbleness, which I think can be referred to as true love, because of which other facets of love are manifested. A person filled with pride cannot show the characteristics of love that the Bible talks about or the way God wants us to love. Love and pride cannot go together—you will have one or the other.

I recall a story once narrated by a pastor from the church that we used to attend in North India. I was very young at that time, maybe in middle school, but even now I remember that story as it had made a big impact on me. It explains the limits of human love. The story was about a mother and her child. When I had recently shared the story to Mr. Vijay Kumar, the one who helped me in writing this book by sharing his opinion and thoughts, he told me that it was actually the story of monkeys; nevertheless the message remains the same. The story goes as follows:

Mother and child, on their way somewhere, falls in a well. Then it starts to rain. The water in that well keeps rising. As it does, the mother tries to protect the child naturally. She tries to keep the child from drowning. Then still, as the water rises, she lifts the child up and holds him high above the water. Still the water rises. She puts him on her shoulders and then on her head. But then when the water covers the mother's mouth and nose and she feels that she might also drown, then she puts the child down and stands on that child to save herself. I know when people hear this, especially the mothers, they may not agree. But just think about this deeply. What that preacher was trying to say was that human love has limits, conditions; when you reach that limit your love can stop. I am a mother myself so when I think about that story, no matter how much I want to deny doing something like that, still in my heart I know it can happen. That is human nature. We tend to think of ourselves first. I think many of us have experienced that at some point in our lives not necessarily in mother-child relationship but could be in other relationships also. I can give several examples, but I would rather not as I pretty much feel people know what I am trying to say.

Does any kind of human love or anyone love without reason or without expecting something in return? We always expect something in return at some point. We might think we do not, but deep down if we are true to ourselves we know we do expect something whether we say it out loud or not. We have a threshold beyond which we cannot tolerate anymore. We fail to acknowledge that fact until we are in a situation like that of the above-mentioned story. Of course there are always exceptions_ because, i.e, when we portray God's love in us. A lot of times we say we cannot live without someone we love, but when that person is not there anymore, we still live even though we claimed otherwise and life goes on. For those who really cannot live then we have psychiatric facilities for them diagnosing them with serious depression. I do agree it is not easy to live then. One may even feel life is not worth living anymore, but the fact is life does not stop for someone; one has to live for oneself, many times for the sake of others. Love hurts whether we accept it or not; still we cannot help but fall in love. Many poems and songs have been written referring to that as "sweet pain."

The only love from which we can expect joy is in God's love, i.e., only if we love the way Scriptures teach us to love. That is because God's love is unconditional and has no limits. God can forgive anything and everything. He takes us back no matter what, where we are, what we have done. He forgives and starts out with a clean slate provided our hearts are pure and true in his sight. God loves us whether we love him or not. Romans 5:5 says, ", because God's love has been poured into our hearts through the Holy Spirit that has been given to us." His love is selfless, forgiving, that is why when we experience his love in our lives, our lives are completely transformed. Then our lives have new meaning—we become complete, happy, joyful, and content. We then even have a forgiving spirit. We tend to become generous and compassionate, and love people unconditionally, which is way different from the love we see around us. We learn to absorb hurts too, because Jesus is continuously healing them. The truth is it's not we but Jesus loving people through us. No more pride is left in us.

Have you ever heard of someone telling you to love your enemies? Jesus tells us to do that by doing that in action. It is not easy to do that; actually it is impossible to do on our own, but with the love of God in us it is possible. So when we obey and do what Jesus tells us to do, then we will experience joy that no one can give or take away. We will live a life that will then be a living testimony for God and pleasing to him. We can show that kind of love only if we have God's love in us, which comes through personal encounter with God that makes us experience his unconditional love. It's only then that we can share and portray the love that is described in 1 Corinthians 13:4–8: "Love is patient; love is kind; love is not envious or boastful or arrogant or rude. It does not insist on its own way; it is not irritable or resentful; it does not rejoice in wrongdoing, but rejoices in the truth. It bears all things, believes all things, hopes all things, endures all things. Love never ends."

One of my favorite gospel singers and pastors, Wilson George, has written and sung a beautiful song in Hindi, the lyrics of which is based on the

Scriptures, but I have translated in English as close as possible. This reads as follows:

> Everyone loves their own loved ones in this
>     world
> But Jesus teaches us to love even others /
>     enemies
>
> If someone slaps on one cheek then turn
>     your other cheek too
> if someone takes you one mile forcibly then
>     you go two miles
> everyone here gives everything to their own
>     loved ones
> but Jesus teaches to give everything to oth-
>     ers too
>
> Whoever gives thorns to you, fill their bos-
>     om with flowers
> Jesus has forgiven you, you too forgive
>     others
> everyone forgives the sins of their own
>     loved ones
> but Jesus teaches us to forgive even our
>     enemies.

# Judging Others Can Give Good Results Too

Judging others gives us pleasure—a feeling of pride—which makes us feel we are better than others. So we often try to judge people knowingly or unknowingly, at which time we don't even pause to think what effect our words will have on other people. We could be sending a message of hurt, rejection, worthlessness, etc., without thinking of the serious consequences of our actions. Of course not everybody will be affected in a negative way, but most people will because we are born to be appreciated.

We only judge people when we think of ourselves as higher than others, or in other words when we are proud of ourselves. Scripture says God hates pride. Repeatedly it is written it leads us to destruction. Those who listen escape from the disaster and those who do not listen experience the disaster. God does not do anything without warning us first, but there are many people who are filled with pride and ignore those warnings.

One of the deadly things that pride can do is to stop us from listening—good or bad, right or wrong. Even if we know the truth, we refuse to accept; and even if we accept, we make sure no matter what we still decide to keep that as a secret.

One day a great servant of God told me my name will not be there in the Book of Life in heaven. He even gave reference for me to read, Revelation 3:5. I was so much hurt but still was curious to know what that verse had said. So as soon as I reached home, I started reading that and I read that multiple times only to find out that it said exactly opposite to what that servant of God had said concerning me. I was kind of disappointed but also happy; weird, right? I thought maybe he meant to say the other way; it was just a slip of tongue. But still I was totally taken by surprise as I had never given a thought on that until then, but it certainly made me think about a lot of things, which then made me read the whole chapter. I do not know why or what made him say that, especially if he did mean it. I wanted to get mad but could not because of four reasons. First of all, it was spoken by one of God's servants who served him for so many years. Second, I was acquainted with him personally through someone that I knew.

Third, he was quite old; I had to respect his age, his experience, his knowledge of the Bible. And lastly, it was a question of forgiveness. I had forgiven him because I knew it is only God who can judge a person. But are we allowed to judge somebody or pass judgment on somebody whom we hardly know? Or even if we did know, aren't many of us like that? We are quick to condemn or judge someone else. In Matthew chapter 7:1–5 Jesus talks about judging others: it basically says we do not have any right to judge, that's something only God can do. There is a proverb, "Do not judge a book from the cover of the book." In other words, we need to look in people's hearts and mind before we come to any kind of conclusion, which no human being can do, and the only person who can do that is God, as people can be deceived easily.

The above incidence made me feel ashamed of myself. I felt disappointed to know that people cannot see Jesus living in me. What kind of born-again believer am I? It made me think that I have to set things right. I have to live a life where and when people can say, "Yes, Jesus lives in her." I was thinking where I had gone wrong, what it is that I did not do right that someone could actually say that. At this point, I felt I still have to go a long way, have to do a lot in life, bring a lot of changes in me, for which I need grace and power of God, for which I am praying for a while now. Not that I have the desire to prove that that person is wrong about me, but it has given insight to me that I have to work really hard to achieve God's purpose for me and to be right with God.

When we are in heaven, I am sure we will be surprised to meet people who are there whom we thought will not be there, or to find out that the people whom we had thought will be there are not there. It is because we as humans are limited in our perception to see and accept the reality; no matter how much we claim to know another person, we still may not know. But we cannot say about God like that because—he knows the ins and outs of our lives, hearts, and minds, that is why when he makes the decision of our lives, we do not understand and have no choice but to accept that.

The heart is wicked; it can devise and think of things that can be anything from good to bad, and it has the capability to hide the most wicked secrets from anyone and everyone depending on the person. We choose to tell people what we want to tell the other person no matter how close we are to that person—that is human nature; nobody can do anything about that. We can hide anything we want from other people but we cannot hide from God because he knows everything he is everywhere no matter where we are, wherever we go. As it says in Psalms 139:7. "Whither shall I go from thy spirit? or whither shall I flee from thy presence?" God searches the inner depths of our hearts. So next time someone passes judgment on us, let us train ourselves not to react with anger but instead try looking in ourselves. It will make us think of things that we never thought before; in fact it might help us to get rid of that invisible pride that we might have. But just always remember one thing—that God is our ultimate judge. Matthew 7:1–2 says, "Judge not, that ye be not judged. For with what judgment ye judge, ye shall be judged:" But if you tend to be judged and you take it in the right or godly perspective, it can do good to you as a child of God.

It is so easy to wander away from God because of the false enticements of this world. The temptations are too many, and pride can make you feel nothing is wrong with anything.

# Blessings and Sufferings Accompany God's Love

I was reflecting upon my life before Jesus came into my heart. People used to call and think of me as the dumbest person—they basically said I do not know anything or cannot do anything, about which they were right. I think even my parents used to worry and say, "We do not know how she will survive in this world." But when Jesus took hold of my life, he changed everything. He made me from zero to hero. Everywhere I had a name for myself—I was not the dumb person anymore. He gave me wisdom, knowledge, skills, talents in every field that I never had before. I thanked God for that with all my heart. I was willing to give all the credit to God whose grace was upon my life. Everywhere I used to write, "With God I am hero, without God I am zero," as it was engraved on my heart.

People were right; I did not belong to my earthly family but belonged to God's family. When I had joined nursing, I was the top student, but people thought it was all because of my parents as they were employees in that hospital. They thought that was the reason for me to get all that recognition, special treatment, and favor from everyone. I was known by my parent's name in the beginning; but before I finished my first year of college, my parents were known by my name. What I mean to say is I had a name for myself, people recognized and acknowledged me for who I was, and so I was known by my own name. God exalted me in ways I never imagined even though my relationship with Him then was not that deep. Still I had trusted him to take care of me completely. I had given him the driver's seat in the luxurious car that he had given me to drive—no cares, no worries, no tears. I was totally enjoying the ride to the places he would take me where I had never been before.

Everything that I did—I excelled. I was an all-rounder be it in studies or extracurricular activities. People used to give me time off to do artwork for the hospital as by then people had labeled me as an artist. I am sure there might have been better artists than me but my talents were accompanied by God's grace. But then things started to change. *Pride* stepped into my life without my knowledge. I had forgotten where I came from, had forgotten the slavery I was in, that God had set me free and had lifted me up. I took his grace, mercy, and love for granted because pride had me thinking it was all because of me—about me—when it was all because of him, about him. When that happens, God steps aside; he does not want to be near you.

It took twenty-some years for me to realize that I had slowly pushed him to the backseat of my car that he had given me. I had drifted away from God to whom once I had submitted myself on my free will, as I would not admit the fact that I had pride. I was trapped in Satan's web that he carefully had weaved for me. As I said before, Satan is very subtle. He makes you think and feel that everything is right until one day you find out that everything is wrong. But I am happy that finally I made the right choice, accepted my mistake, truly repented; as such God forgave me without questioning or condemning, which makes me want to love him even more. Now when I think about it, my heart and my eyes gets filled with tears and I ask myself, *How could I even do that?* And then I ask God, *How could you let me drift away like that? Why didn't you stop me? Why did you wait for twenty years to reprove me?* When I think about it again, it all comes back to the choices that we make. He does not want to take away that freedom of freewill from us.

Once as a church we were watching a movie about making choices or decisions. The moral of the story was whatever decisions we make have consequences, good or bad, depending on our decisions. The decisions that we make without godly counsel could always end up in bad consequences. Because the decisions then are made based on human knowledge, logic, and understanding, which has limitations, as we only see the present because we are limited in our perception of tomorrow. On the other hand, if we make decisions based on godly counsel (God is aware of the past, the present, and the future), then we can never regret because we then will surely have good consequences. God was waiting for me to make the right decision, to realize my mistake, my sin, and he wanted me to repent. So what was my sin? Prideful heart, big time, which I was not willing to accept for a long time; and even more than that, I was not willing to say and think that pride is something that God hates, which is repeatedly said many times in the Scriptures.

Pride destroyed my life, took away all the blessings, the joy, the peace, the security—everything that I had. Of course I had enjoyed life, but only for that moment because that enjoyment did not last long as that happiness came from the world. I was great in the eyes of people—I was a top student, artist, actress, choreographer, writer, producer, director, etc., everything—but in my heart I felt I was nothing. I was emptied; something that I had that was so precious to me had gone out without my knowledge or consent. I am pretty sure I would not have let that go had I realized what I was losing. See, that is how cunningly Satan works. He knows very well how to get us when we are most vulnerable, the easiest way being through pride, which stops us from looking beyond ourselves.

The God that I had submitted to once, the God that I had accepted on my free will, the God that I used to say knows what is best for me, the God that I wanted to depend on for everything, that God I was leaving, yet I was not even aware of it. There is a song, "*Come Thou Fount of Every Blessing,*" which is one of my favorites, in which it is said, "Lord I always have a feeling that I am vulnerable to stray from the God that I love; so, please take my heart and seal it for your kingdom."

It is so easy to wander away from God because of the false enticement of this world; the temptations are too many and pride can make you feel nothing wrong with anything. That is why I personally think pride can be considered as one great sin, and I fully agree. "Pride goeth before destruction" (Proverbs 20:16). When it steps in your life, it destroys you and your life before you even realize, before you can stop, and sometimes it is just too late. But still for me God was very faithful, he still is, and I am sure he will be. He kept his side of the promise, he kept his covenant with me, he did not forsake me. He still loved me, blessed me with all the blessings that I did not deserve. He still talked to me, helped me when I needed his help and guidance and asked for it.

In our church we sing one song "Your Grace Is Enough," which I like very much except the part when we sing as if we are telling God to remember his promise, his people. I cannot sing that part because I feel that it is not God who forgets, but it is us who don't keep the promise and forget him.

For those twenty years of my life that I was trapped in Satan's web, God still protected me. He made me fall to a certain point then he just grabbed me and pulled me out in ways that I will never understand, for which I will ever be grateful to him. After all that I did, certainly I did not deserve his mercy, love, forgiveness, yet he did that anyway even though he did let me go through many trials, which I thought were not fair at the time. Maybe he wanted me to feel the pain and agony that I had put him through when I had drifted away from him, or maybe he wanted to refine me like gold or silver so that I will never ever get tarnished again, because now what I feel about myself is so different. After enduring through those trials, I have grown to be much stronger in faith than I was ever before. This is my second life that I received from

God, which I owe it all to him. There is no place for Satan in my life now and I am sure even he knows that this time, he will have to pass through my God to reach me, which is not only difficult but impossible. Now I realize it was a good thing that I went through the bitter experience and trial with my son so I could become much stronger in Christ. See, if we get things the easy way, we do not appreciate and value them as much. But something we persevere for and worked hard or suffer for to get, we obviously will value that very much.

When the first time I had accepted God just because he had answered my prayer, even though for the time being I was happy and in that excitement had said to him "you are my God," maybe I did not mean with the passion and love that I have now. But now after enduring through the trial and suffering with my son, now when I say to him that I accept him, it is so different. It is not just my mouth that says, it is my whole self—100 percent of me—that says, "You are my God; I am completely yours." He knows this time that I really mean it and this time I too am sure that I mean it. That is what God wanted from me—a total surrender, sincere repentance of my sins, to give up my pride which was a barrier between me and him, for me to understand myself, know his purpose of my life on this earth, the things that I am supposed to do, to have the joy of living. God wanted me to live a life like him, show people when he lives through us what a transformation takes place in our lives, how the changes that take place in us can affect ours and others' lives around us. It is now my greatest desire that people will see those changes in my life and my family's life so that my life will become a testimony for this world. It gives me great joy to do his will and work.

As you read this, I hope and pray that God will help you give up your *pride*, if you have any, and then he will reveal his purpose for your life. There is nothing more joyful than finding out what you are living for in this world. Is your life just getting born, grow, and die? Or is it something more than that? What you are called for? What do you need to do? Are you doing what you are called for? Because only then your life will be fulfilling. You will then have the joy and peace that God promises that no one can give, neither can anyone take away. And then even when you die you will die peacefully without fear knowing that you have an eternal life with him and can boldly stand in front of him.

# Accepting and Doing God's Will

How much pride Jesus should have had when Jesus was on this earth as a human being, knowing that he is the Son of God, creator of this universe, with all the power of healing, raising people from the dead, ability to perform various miracles? Even then Jesus was humble enough to get humiliated, beaten up for our sins just to fulfill the purpose of God to die on that cross—the most painful death that anybody could ever imagine. It brings tears into my eyes, giving me goose bumps just to think how he might have felt when that one nail went through his hand—I cannot even think or imagine the rest. And that, too, for whom—to save people like me and you from going into eternal fire. Why? Why? Why do that for people who are not even willing to acknowledge and accept him as their savior? Can you even comprehend the depth of his love for unworthy people like us? Can you imagine how much happiness it will give to God when people will turn toward Him? He will think that the price that his son, Jesus, paid on that cross did not get wasted and it was well worth it.

I always like to relate everything to my life. I try to tell my children how much I had suffered, what all I went through to raise them especially since no one was there to help me at that time. Everything then was new to me when I first came to the USA—new country, new marriage, new people, new family, new job, new environment, but even then I had survived. It was God's strength and grace which I had failed to acknowledge at that time. Of course, I had made several mistakes which I realize now as I was dealing with issues using more of my own logic, knowledge and understanding which now I know was very limited. I had thought it was my strength and so had felt proud of myself. Now when I look back the way I had handled the situations, I'm myself amazed and feel there was no way I could have done that but the fact remains, I then had done. The secret behind of which I now understand which was that God was with me, who had carried me through. Even though I was not faithful to him, still he had remained faithful to me just because I had accepted him as my Father in my teenage years. Without him I would have been lost. It is not easy to raise kids especially these days. I keep telling them of the pain we have to go through to make them happy but they do not seem to understand, maybe some do, and some do not. They think that it is their birthright to receive everything, being our children, and that it is our job to raise them and provide everything that they want or need. Maybe to some extent I agree they are right. What they fail to understand is that we do not have to do that, there are other options, but we do that out of our love toward them because we think and feel that they are a part of us, belong to us, which they take for granted. They take advantage of our love as we do of our Almighty God. We need to understand God does not have to love us the way he does; in fact we do not deserve his love at all. What are we—just dust; we came from dust and we will go back to dust when our days are over. But God has loved us so much that he has given us the privilege to be his children, through believing in his son Jesus Christ to have eternal life. So let us not take his love for granted but instead be grateful and obedient to his commandments, so that our lives will be blessed and prosperous. Let us live a life like Jesus did without any pride.

There should be no room for the word "pride" in our lives or hearts. If Jesus had become so humble and lowly in spite of having all the power, then how much more humble we should be since we do not even have what Jesus had, not even the designation of being the Son of God. Let the world know about Christ living in us through our lives, behavior, love, and compassion. Let us not boast ourselves, as the saying goes, "When we sing our own praises usually the tune goes very high." For me, I want my God to boast about me—that will be the greatest compliment I can get as a human being.

God had enriched me again with many talents —improved my skills in every field—sometimes it becomes difficult to choose which one to use for his glory. I used to be so proud of myself of all the talents which had made me forget the one who had given me those talents until he reminded me through painful ways, as I was so engrossed in myself, closed myself so much that nothing could make me realize that I was going in the wrong direction. I am glad God did not let me fall to the bottom of the pit; he pulled me out before I did that, and today I am still alive to tell about it—the deliverance he gave me just because I finally realized and accepted my mistakes, my sins, my pride and eventually repented. Today I can also include myself in the list of the happiest people in the world because I feel free. God readily took all my worries, my problems, my burdens on his shoulders once I decided to let go of it, which he wanted to do for a long time, and so once again I gave him the driver seat and decided to relax in the backseat of my car that he had given to me, feeling free of all the cares and worries— this time for life.

My son often tells me I read and pray so much, then why I still worry about him especially when he comes home very late at night. No matter what I say, he does not seem to understand that I am not worried about him the way he thinks, as my God already promised that he will take care of my children, he will teach them so they will be prosperous, but what I want to show him is that I love him, I cannot sleep when he is out somewhere in the middle of the night when he should be sleeping. Often, he tells me that is the time when most of the troubled kids are out on the street who really need to hear that there is someone (God) who loves them unconditionally with which I do agree. But still it is very difficult as a parent to explain to your child something that you agree with yet seems you feel you disagree...mainly because you are concerned of your child's safety and welfare. Ever since God gave me the promise about my children, I have stopped worrying about them, but I do not want them to think that I do not care about them or love them. My children have the best father they could have, both in the physical sense and spiritual sense—what more could I want? It is a promise from someone (God) who never breaks promises.

I know that he will never leave us in the midst of life's storms but carry us safely to the other end of the shore. We just need to make sure that we do not let that pride make a way into our heart or lives; keep our eyes and ears open so we can recognize the subtleness of Satan who is waiting to devour us especially through pride. It says, "Resist the devil and he will flee from you" (James 4:7). It is good to always remember this verse.

Make your life worth living and see that many are blessed because of your life on this earth, as Jesus showed from his life that even after more than 2,000 years we still talk and acknowledge Jesus who did something for mankind, something so great that whoever accepts the truth becomes a debtor to his grace and love. He is the one and only way to heaven and eternal life.

# Faith That My Son Taught Me

Ever since I started to walk with God, I have been trying to attend these prayer meetings regularly that we have as part of our church activity and I try hard not to miss them even one. It is like keeping a date with your beloved—I feel I will miss something very special if I do not. So, anyway, during one of those meetings I was saying to God, "God, you know this is the best place where you and I can talk freely without anybody disturbing or without having to explain to anybody what I am doing." Suddenly thoughts came to me flowing like a river that I felt I needed to add them here in this chapter.

It is again about my son. We had an argument, we always do, and I feel these are the only times lately that we talk to each other without any restraints. He always gives me something to think about, or I should say keeps my brain working. He has always been a very outgoing person, going out of his way to help people in need, maybe one of the reasons because of which it was so difficult for me to keep him to stay inside the house.

I recall one incident one Sunday when my husband had gone early with my daughter and so my son ended up driving us both to church. On the way someone had a flat tire, which I noticed after my son had stopped our car on the shoulder of the highway. Before I could even figure out anything, my son had already stepped out of the car and started helping that stranger who was trying to change a flat tire alone. I did try to talk my son out of helping that stranger, which he did not listen anyway, for which I'm glad.

As I watched my son helping that stranger in bitter, cold weather without even having any gloves or winter coat, I realized what I was trying to do was wrong. I was trying to stop my son from doing something good for the two wrong reasons that I had felt right at that time. One was because we were getting late to church, and the other one was because of my past experience in a similar situation where my husband had been injured trying to help a stranger—that, too, in a church parking lot. But in my heart I did really want my son to help that person, which my son was already doing, and I was happy he did not listen to me.

See, lot of times we as parents think whatever we say and tell our children to do is always right. But not quite, especially in situations like this because parents see and think what children do not see or care. Selfishness gets in the way. I was more concerned about my son's safety based on my previous experience, which later I realized it was wrong of me to think and pass a judgment that way. By the time we reached church, the service was almost over, but I did not feel sorry for having missed the church service as I was really happy for my son had helped that person. What I am trying to say is that we need to see the world through the eyes of children; maybe that is why it says in Bible that if we need to enter the kingdom of God we need to be like little children. I was so much conscious of going to church on time that I did not pay much attention to what is being said repeatedly in church, but my son was actually following the Scriptures.

It was a great eye-opening experience for me; we can really learn a lot from our children. We think we need to teach our children—it is, of course, our responsibility as parents—but we should not forget that God has placed those children in our lives so we can equally learn from them very valuable lessons every day. We many times underestimate our children's abilities and try to limit their potential.

For some time now my son was working at Payless shoe store during his summer holidays. I was kind of happy at least he is not wasting his time not doing anything, though I would have been much happier if he had decided to take some summer classes. For me education is very important and I wanted to instill in my children's hearts the importance of it in their lives. I used to tell them that everything in this world will come and go and people can take it away from them, but the knowledge, wisdom, and education is something that nobody can take away. So I used to tell them that they should study hard, gain knowledge and wisdom as much as they can while we are there to support them, whether or not they take that advice is up to them.

Anyway, my son told me that he is planning to quit his job as he decided to go to Central Bible College in Missouri. At first I felt my heart had stopped just at the thought that he was thinking of going away from home even though I have been praying about it for months when he had casually expressed his desire to do that. I had even received an answer again during another prayer meeting when our pastor's sister-in-law shared something. She had said we think we know our children, but we really do not know them, especially how much potential they have; we underestimate their abilities based on our experience. It is our job as parents to see that we do not limit their abilities, their growth, but rather guide and encourage them in the right way rather—God's way. That actually helped me to decide that it will be the right thing to do for my son, but still I had the desire that somehow he will change his mind and stay here with us. Here my son was telling me that he wanted to go to Bible college, eventually do God's work, and I was kind of discouraging him.

I of course had valid reason for doing so, as my son had told me with so much confidence before that he wanted to do dentistry and he had wasted one year of his life going to college for that. I was trying to make the decision based on his past experience, not knowing and accepting the changes that had taken place in my son's life through Jesus. I did not want him to go in ministry for the wrong reasons. I explained to him about the pros and cons of choosing that profession, which he pretty much knew, but even after all that when I saw that he was determined, I asked him if he will get the admission in the Bible college, because as far as I knew he had not done anything toward the admission process. So when I asked him about that, he said he does not know whether he will get the admission yet, and he was telling me all this just a week before the classes were scheduled to start.

You could imagine the frustration that it was causing me. Here my son was telling me that he was quitting a job to do something that he could not give a guarantee of any kind. I did not quite know what to say; then finally, as a worldly mother, I advised him to quit the job after he is sure that he will be accepted in the Bible college. My son's immediate reply brought tears in my eyes when he said with so much confidence, "Mama, I walk by faith not by sight." I was speechless, I felt what a transformation had taken place in his life; it should have been my place to tell him that, but instead he is telling me. I could not argue with him anymore and decided to let him go even though the thought of separation was breaking my heart. I then just prayed to God to fulfill his desire as he had totally surrendered himself to God for his needs. And my son actually quit his job and went to Missouri with just a few of his belongings before he even knew that he will get admission—which actually strengthened my faith in God. I did not have any fear anymore for my son and really admired my son deeply for the decision he had made in spite of us not encouraging or supporting him.

Similar experience I had with my daughter Nikeeta also, who took a step further as she is even farther away from home. People say I'm very brave. If someone had said that to me a couple of years back, I would not have agreed; but today I cannot deny that because I know who is with me today and who is holding my future—I believe in every promise that I received from God. Deep down my heart longs for my children; my son is twelve to fourteen hours away from home when he never left home all these years, but still I knew I did the right thing. He is where God intended him to be. It is written, God never tests you beyond your strength (1 Corinthians 10:13). Besides, my son is going to do his work—what better thing to do in this world? At first I was disappointed as I wanted him to do something in medical field just so that we do not have problem getting jobs in the future. But God had different plans for him, as every time I prayed everything that happened slowly confirmed that he has chosen him for his work.

Even today that incidence brings tears in my eyes thinking how God could pick someone for his glory who belonged to someone as disobedient as me in his sight. I cannot comprehend God's unconditional love, the decisions he makes for our lives when we surrender ourselves to him completely. He wanted me to dedicate my son for his service and he had also prepared his heart to do that, so I did not have any choice but let go of him. I sure miss my son, as I am and forever will be his mother, but now I understand my son is not created to be confined to us, our own family, but that he has a bigger mission in life. He has to complete the work of God that he has been called for, and I thank him for choosing my son for his purpose.

I was thinking what Mary, mother of Jesus, must have gone through when Jesus had started his ministry, seeing her son suffer and crucified on the cross. I can understand the pain that she might have felt, how much God might have strengthened her to endure everything. It was not that Mary did not care about her firstborn son, but she was told and knew it had to be that way. I do not know where my son will end up, but I pray that wherever he will be, he will shine as the light of God's love. God had reminded and comforted me by saying, "I have chosen him. Do not worry." Sometimes I even take pride in that though knowing fully well it is not the right thing to do. Of all the people God could have chosen, he chose my son to do his work. Looking back, at my son's life-style, what is more interesting is that my son has accepted his will for him.

See what I mean how easy pride can get you? That is why it says in Proverbs, "When pride cometh, then cometh shame:" (Proverbs 11:2). Even though I agree a sin is a sin no matter what, but still I feel pride can be considered as the greatest sin, as it leads you to commit all other sins.

Pride lives in you as a parasite, destroys your body without your consent, yet you are not even aware of it.

*Pride* and *proud* can be two different things, especially in other languages. They give different meanings, and it might even seem okay to be proud. I had a discussion regarding this with my pastor as usual. But the fact remains—God hates pride whether it is good or bad; he does not want us to have it. A lot of times we say the word "pride" can be okay, depending on how we use it, especially when we use it in a sentence like, "I am proud of my daughter's talent as a dancer." There does not seem anything wrong with that, not in the beginning at least, but if we keep repeating that a few times, think of the effect it might have either on the person who is saying it or the person who is hearing it. It can eventually lead to have pride in somebody that God does not like. Why give chance for the devil to even enter by keeping the door wide open? He is already sneaky enough to come in with the doors being closed.

1 Thessalonians 5:21–22 says, "Abstain from all appearance of evil"; in other words it advises us to stay away even at the appearance of evil. I don't think God ever used *proud* when he spoke about somebody. I am sure God must have been proud of many people in Bible, especially Jesus,

when he finished doing what he was supposed to do. We should always pray that pride never steps in our lives. Now I get so scared when I think what pride can do because of the destruction that it had caused in my life. Now I often wonder, Why do we take pride in anything anyway, because we do not even have control over our own next breath that we take; then how can we even think of taking pride in other things in life? But we still do knowingly or unknowingly, don't we? It does not make sense, does it?

# God Loves Humility

A couple of years back, my husband told me that Ravi Zacharias, one of the well-known preachers, is coming to a church in Michigan close to our house and that he had just written one more new book. I used to read a lot of books before—secular ones. I have read many books both in English and Hindi written by many different authors, but my favorite in English was Agatha Christie and Nevil Shute, and in Hindi—Gulshan Nanda. I loved mysteries and adventures. Just a few years back the one book that I liked reading was *Harry Potter*, even though I felt gross reading that, but I had to appreciate the way it was written—the imagination of that author was incredible. I did not always read books just for the sake of reading but rather used to look for something—something that would appeal to me, that would make me think, that would inspire me to do something. Same thing with movies or anything that I watched—I never watched just for the sake of watching or killing time or because I was getting bored. I would always look for something, many times without any clue as to what I am looking.

Whenever I read Agatha Christie and Gulshan Nanda books, it would inspire me to write, especially when I read Agatha Christie's biography. It was somewhere in my subconscious mind that I will someday write a book but never ever thought or dreamed of writing any religious books, as I myself never liked anything to do with religion let alone read (or write) anything about them. But after experiencing God in my life and reading the Bible, I found that there is no other book in this world which is more interesting than that. It has everything—love, crimes, mysteries, adventures, etc., above all, the way to salvation, and life after death which, I think, no other book in this world talks about. Everything in the Bible that we read speaks back to us. It is a living word because our God is living—no other book can do that. It gives new life to you.

Even now I do not read many religious books though I would very much like to, as I myself have a list of books which I first need to finish writing. It is not easy to write books as anything else, especially religious books, because we are writing something that only we are convinced about—about God. Even then we are willing to boldly proclaim something that other people cannot see with their physical eyes, which can create conflicts in people. That is because there will be no scientific theory or evidence that we can give which can satisfy people's curiosity and which will be able to explain our experience in a way that people can understand that makes us write. Anyway, so when I came to know about Ravi Zacharias's new book, I had mixed feelings of excitement and disappointment.

As I remembered about a year back, I had borrowed one of his books from my pastor to read because the name of that book had got my attention when I was surfing through all the books he had in his house. It said *Can Man Live without God?* It seemed pretty interesting so I borrowed it to read. When I brought that home and started reading, it seemed like it was a never-ending book. It took too long for me to read. And then to understand what I read, I needed a dictionary. Maybe that book was meant for theological students or for people with great IQ or vocabulary. It was very well written, had a lot of quotations, references, and showed that even that author had read a lot of books himself. But after a few months that I had finished reading that book, I tried to recall what was written in that book, but to my disappointment, after all that hard work, all I could remember was just two things. One was about a story of torturing a chicken and the other one was a song written by one of the famous American folk rock singers, Harry Chapin's wife, which was sung by him, that had touched my heart. That song will surely touch many people's hearts especially the fathers of this generation. It's a song called *"Cat's in the Cradle."* Most of you might have heard it already, but if you have never heard it, then you can hear it on the Internet on YouTube.

This song is about a father who is occupied with his business so much that he does not have time to spend with his kid. The son yearns for his father's company and love while he makes him his model, even though the father constantly gives excuses and promises to be with him, which creates a distance between them.

Of course, he provides his son with material things that he could buy with money. Then as time passes, they switch roles. Now the father, being old, yearns for his grown-up son's company. But the son, who is now grown up like his father, has learned a valuable lesson and does not hesitate to politely say to his father that he cannot spend time with him since he is very busy with his job and would rather show his love by spending time with his kids who are sick. As we read, we feel sorry for the father who is now regretting not spending time with his son when he wanted him to or show his love, thus creating a huge vacuum between them that could not be filled.

It is a beautiful, meaningful, heart-aching song that gives a valuable lesson to those who want to learn, not just for fathers but also for mothers, especially now that more and more mothers are working outside the homes, whether it's by force or choice. It just pierces our hearts right through, especially when we think how much quality time we actually spend with our children or how we show our love toward them. Do we even take time to teach our children the word of God—to fear, obey and love God, which the Lord has commanded us to do as parents?

Nothing in this world matters more than love; and when our love is preceded by God's love only then can there be wonderful results. I could not recall anything else in that book no matter how much I tried—even though I wanted to be able to recall at least little bit more, as I had spent so much time reading that book. I was so much frustrated and angry with myself for not being able to recall anything else. So when I heard he had written a new book, *Has Christianity Failed You?*, I was not that thrilled even though the topic was very inviting. Still I had the desire to attend his meeting since people talked about him so much, about his wonderful messages. Also I had got off from my work that Sunday, even though it was my weekend to work especially without my requesting off. So I thought maybe God really wants me to attend this meeting. I did not even have a ride because my husband was working that day but even that arrangement was also made without my effort. As such I was really convinced that God had something in store for me.

Even then I was not very excited to attend this meeting, but still before going I said to God, "God I am only going there because I feel it is your desire and I know for sure that you want me to go. I certainly do not want to go there for the wrong reasons—to find out whether he is a famous preacher or not, or to criticize him, or to even give a certificate to him from my side how good of a preacher he is, but I really want to hear what you will speak through him to me." That little prayer changed my attitude toward this preacher and to go for this meeting that I reluctantly was going to attend.

I felt very happy from the beginning the worship started to the end as I felt God's presence so strong throughout the whole service. Ravi Zacharias obviously was a very well-spoken, eloquent preacher, which people had rightfully acknowledged, and he certainly kept everyone interested to hear what he had to say, with some humorous jokes throughout his preaching. After hearing him, I felt, *Wow, awesome preaching.* I had to acknowledge he was a wonderful preacher—this person has so much knowledge, so much intelligence, so much talent. How can God give all these things to just one person? But the thing that brought tears to my eyes was something that God spoke through him about this book that I was writing. It was about *pride* which he said is the biggest hurdle between human and God. It basically confirmed what I had written already.

After that he said and talked about a lot of other things that interested me, but I appreciated the fact that in spite of all the recognition, he still portrayed himself to be a down-to-earth person; he still loved and acknowledged God as the creator. He was willing to admit and appreciate other human beings, their values, especially when he told about the incidence of a man who was staying in the same hotel with him. He said about the man he was talking that, that man's house got burnt completely in the fire that day, that is why he was staying in that hotel with his family. He had told him his story about how he had lost everything that he earned and owned throughout his life in the fire, but still that man was asking Ravi Zacharias about his ministry and inquiring about his whereabouts. And then he said he couldn't understand how peaceful this man was; here there was somebody who had lost everything that he owned, for which he must have worked hard throughout his life to possess, yet in that situation he was not sad or worried but instead concerned about someone else's whereabouts and ministry. And then he went on to add that if he was in his place, he was not sure if he would have done the same thing.

Then Ravi Zacharias said that even though he preaches and teaches these great sermons, when it comes to doing, he finds it difficult to do it; and he was humble enough to admit that in front of thousands of people who respect him so much and even want to follow in his footsteps. He said here was an ordinary man who is showing everything in action what the great preachers have preached, who may not even get noticed by anybody. I was very much impressed the way Ravi Zacharias reacted to this unknown man's actions in spite of being a great preacher. He still is humble enough to appreciate a simple man's act and concern for his ministry. I think God is pleased with such people who can appreciate other human beings that he created, no matter how big or small they are or whether or not they possess anything. Maybe that is why his ministry is so powerful and growing—it is the humility that I think he still has through which he receives grace and blessings for himself, his ministry.

That great service that I did not want to end unfortunately ended, but I thanked God for making me attend that service where he taught me a great lesson. Then I bought his new book, *Has Christianity Failed You?*, came home, and read most of the book. Everything that he had written was very practical. I thought they can be applied to our everyday lives; maybe that is one of the reason his books are so popular. Then of course I read some of his other books and also books from some other well-known authors; most of them were beautifully written. I was thinking—after reading such great books written by great authors like that— who will read my books? But it did not matter any more now because what I was writing was basically my experience with God, which is very different from those "authors," as God deals with everyone on an individual unique way. Since there is no way to tell everyone of all that God has done in my life, I thought of writing in the form of books so that people who are looking for some unanswered questions in their lives may be encouraged by reading this book.

No two experiences with God are or will be the same. We will never get enough time to share God's goodness, our experiences with God in churches or other places, because of the time factor. But through the way of books, with which I chose to share my experiences, at least people can come to know by reading on their own free will and time, at their convenience and pace. Above all, I was told to write and share these things by someone who has redeemed me of my sins and transformed my life completely, which is now worth living. I just wanted to be obedient to his will even though before writing my first book I had argued a lot with God as I did not have a clue as to how to even write a book.

Though I had written a couple of articles, stories, and plays during my college years, I had no idea when it comes to writing a book. I was glad as eventually I yielded myself to him so he could use me to glorify him. That's when he brought the right people in my life who actually helped me to write. See, when we express the desire to do what God calls us for, he makes the paths straight for us and provide the right tools that are necessary to accomplish his purpose.

I sincerely hope and pray that if those who are proud will read this book, and if their attitude can be changed by this book, or somehow this book will convince them that they are proud, giving them the desire to become humble, thus preventing them from losing their blessings, then I will think this book has accomplished its purpose. Because pride is something very difficult for people to get convinced about; for people to accept that as a sin is even difficult, and then to bring people to the point of being humble, it is impossible until God steps in and takes control over, because it is only God who can convict and convince somebody of their pride.

Let me give one example from the book of Daniel—the story of King Nebuchadnezzar, about whom Sister Manisha had talked about pride when once I had requested her to do so. You can read his story in Daniel 4:1–37. The story tells us that King Nebuchadnezzar had a dream about his downfall, which was interpreted by Daniel, yet one day while he was looking at his established kingdom, in verse 30 he says, "The king spake, and said, Is not this great Babylon, that I have built for the house of the kingdom by the might of my power, and for the honour of my majesty?" This clearly portrays the pride that had invaded the king. After that, we read everything happens according to his dream, humiliating him to worse than animals. Then, of course, when he comes back to his senses, he humbles himself, repents, and acknowledges God's power in verse 37, "all whose works are truth, and his ways judgment: and those that walk in pride he is able to abase." Once the king praises and extols God, he forgives King Nebuchadnezzar and reestablishes his kingdom. Then the following chapter,

Daniel 5:1–30 talks about his son Belshazzar who repeats his father's mistakes knowingly and still does not humble himself. So then God does not forgive him and that night itself he gets killed and the story of his life ends—he dies exactly the way Daniel foretold about his death.

If we think about that—that's the story of our lives too. No matter how many stories, testimonies, and experiences of people we hear, we still tend to repeat the same mistakes of our ancestors. Satan is very subtle in taking us to that direction if we are not careful. He knows exactly when we will be vulnerable and he then leaves no chance of getting us.

Many times I get so many thoughts sometimes flowing like a river freely. It's then that I am sure those thoughts could not be mine, sometimes so many that it becomes difficult to put them together. That is when I take help from Sister Manisha from our church because she often speaks what I am thinking about, which then helps me to organize my thoughts and somehow helps me to connect the dots together. She is a wonderful speaker—I often thought it would be nice to speak like her, but I cannot do that. I have to write everything down and many times she helps me to confirm and write my thoughts. It is difficult to comprehend why and how God works, the way he works. The more I think about it, the more I realize that if everyone had same talents of doing things, then how could God use us for different works that he wants to do through us? It was then that I was led to read one of the chapters in Corinthians 12:12–27, regarding building of church. As I read that chapter it started making sense.

We need to understand that church is not just a building made of bricks and mortar constructed beautifully to show to people; rather it is a body of believers who are willing to do the work of God, for God. It is a place where we come together to worship God and get empowered by the Holy Spirit to fulfill the purpose of God, so that when we go out among people who are not believers, we can remain strong in what we believe and thus accomplish his purpose for our lives. We should focus more on beautifying people than beautifying the building. God does not care about the building as much as he cares about the souls that are there in the building and outside. He clearly says in Acts 17:24, "God that made the world and all things therein, seeing that he is Lord of heaven and earth, dwelleth not in temples made with hands;" Yet in another verse, Acts 7:49, he says, "Heaven is my throne, and earth is my footstool: what house will ye build me?"

It speaks loudly that God is not interested in building churches for him but rather to build relationships with human beings. Still we focus on building or making buildings beautiful instead of working to make the relationships beautiful. We have to understand everybody is equally important in building the church. It is compared to our physical body with different parts. For example, the eyes cannot say to the ears, "I am more important than you are," or the hands cannot say to the legs, "I am more important than you are." For the body to function properly, we need all our body parts to work well and to work synchronized. They are all equally important and required to function effectively.

Same thing with the church—various people with different backgrounds, with different talents, make up the church body. For the church to function efficiently, everyone is equally important and everyone needs to work in harmony with each other. Every little thing we do in church for the church is very significant in the sight of God as long as it is done for the glory of God. To do something like that sincerely, we need to have humbleness and a total surrender to God; otherwise it is impossible to do the work and will of God. For that to happen, we need God's spirit to work in us; only then there will not be any pride, jealousy, and we will respect each other for our unique talents no matter how trivial it is. Everything—every little thing—is important for God to build his church. No job is considered menial in his sight, and that is the mentality each one of us should have for the growth of the church, which means there should be no room for pride in our lives, and that can only happen when *Jesus* lives in us, who is the perfect example of humbleness.

It is God's promise, "By humility and the fear of the Lord are riches, honor and life" (Proverbs 22:4). We cannot please God without faith and we cannot have faith without humility. We receive God's blessings only when we are considered humble in God's book. Pride not only destroys our lives but it destroys other people's lives around us. Pride can make us spiritually blind. It can make us go where we don't want to go, make us think what we don't want to think, make us do what we will not want to do otherwise. We need to build ourselves, people in our families, society, and nations which can only happen when we are willing to serve rather than be served just as Jesus Christ showed by his example.

Scripture warns us repeatedly to stay away from having a prideful heart or pride—the original sin, the deadly sin, the most subtle sin, an invisible sin, the greatest sin (?), which is the root cause of all sins. It advises us to save ourselves from getting trapped in the web that Satan has ready for those who are vulnerable to become victims to this pride that God hates, which can give birth to all sins and which is a barrier between God and us. The only way to do that is to keep Jesus in your life and heart. Just remember always and write on your heart permanently in bold letters Proverbs 16:4, "PRIDE GOETH BEFORE DESTRUCTION."

# Index

## A

Abraham
Apostle
Adversary
Acts 7:49, 17:24

## B

Baptism
Bible
believers
blessings
boldness

## C

Choices
Creator
Consent
Commandments
Christian

1 Chronicles 21:17
2 Chronicles 26
1 Corinthians 3:2, 10:13, 13:4–8

# D

David
Daniel 4:30, 37
Deuteronomy 4:36
Disobedience
Destruction
Devil
Dangerous prayer

# E

Excitement
Existence
Excellence
Ephesians 2:8–9,
Ecclesiastes 3:11, 5:5

# F

Forgiveness
Freedom
Fear

# G

Generations

Gifts
Guardian
Genesis 22:12

## H

Holy Spirit
Humility
Heaven
Hospital
Hebrews 13:5

## I

Indian
Israel
Iniquity
Isaiah 42:8, 61:1

## J

Jesus Christ
Johny Lever
Joshua 24:15
John 3:3, 8:12, 14:15,
    15:18
James 4:7, 14,
Job 33:14–17

# K

Knowledge
Kerala
Kingdom
1 Kings 3:12–13

# L

Lucifer
Lepers
Light
Luke 18:16–17

# M

Masters
Marriage
Messages
Moses
Monkeys
Matthew 6:24, 7:1–3,
    28:20, 33
Mark 8:38

# N

Niagara Falls
Nikeeta
Nursing

# O

Outcomes
Opportunities
Obedience

# P

Promises
Parable
Psalms 32:1, 8, 139:7, 8
Proverbs 1:7, 11:2, 16:18, 21:2–4,
    22:4, 6, 23:26, 26:12, 30:5
1st Peter 5:8,

# Q

Questions
Qualifies
Quotes

# R

Ravi Zacharias
Repentance
Religion
Romans 5:5, 8:28, 10:17,
Revelation 3:20, 4:11

# S

Sin

Savior
Satan
Solomon
Salvation
Songs
Speaking in tongues
1st Samuel 17:47

## T

Testimony
Transformation
Talents
1st Thessalonians 5:21–22

## U

Uzziah
United States
Universe

## V

Vanity
Vincent
Vijay Kumar
Victory

## W

Wicked

Wisdom
Wealth

Y

Yield
Yearns

Z

Zechariah
Zero